Landmarks of world literature

Thomas Mann

BUDDENBROOKS

D1049624

Landmarks of world literature

General Editor: J. P. Stern

Dickens: *Bleak House* – Graham Storey
Homer: *The Iliad* – Michael Silk
Dante: *The Divine Comedy* – Robin Kirkpatrick
Rousseau: *Confessions* – Peter France
Goethe: *Faust. Part One* – Nicolas Boyle
Woolf: *The Waves* – Eric Warner
Goethe: *The Sorrows of Young Werther* – Martin Swales
Constant: *Adolphe* – Dennis Wood
Balzac: *Old Goriot* – David Bellos
Mann: *Buddenbrooks* – Hugh Ridley
Homer: *The Odyssey* – Jasper Griffin
Tolstoy: *Anna Karenina* – Anthony Thorlby

FORTHCOMING
Conrad: *Nostromo* – Ian Watt
Camus: *The Stranger* – Patrick McCarthy
García Márquez: *100 Years of Solitude* – Michael Wood
Flaubert: *Madame Bovary* – Stephen Heath
Shikibu: *The Tale of Genji* – Richard Bowring
Sterne: *Tristram Shandy* – Wolfgang Iser

THOMAS MANN

Buddenbrooks

HUGH RIDLEY
University College, Dublin

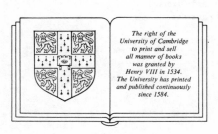

*The right of the
University of Cambridge
to print and sell
all manner of books
was granted by
Henry VIII in 1534.
The University has printed
and published continuously
since 1584.*

CAMBRIDGE UNIVERSITY PRESS

Cambridge
New York   New Rochelle   Melbourne   Sydney

Published by the Press Syndicate of the University of Cambridge
The Pitt Building, Trumpington Street, Cambridge CB2 1RP
32 East 57th Street, New York, NY 10022, USA
10 Stamford Road, Oakleigh, Melbourne 3166, Australia

First published 1987

Printed in Great Britain at
the University Press, Cambridge

British Library cataloguing in publication data

Ridley, Hugh
Thomas Mann : Buddenbrooks.–
(Landmarks of world literature).
1. Mann, Thomas. Buddenbrooks
I. Title II. Series
833′.912   PT2625.A44B9

Library of Congress cataloguing in publication data

Ridley, Hugh
Thomas Mann : Buddenbrooks.
(Landmarks of world literature)
Bibliography.
1. Mann, Thomas, 1875–1955. Buddenbrooks. I. Title.
II. Series.
PT2625.A44B896 1987   833′.912   87–15067

ISBN 0 521 32813 6 hard covers
ISBN 0 521 31697 9 paperback

GG

For Guy and Simon

There are some trees Watson, which grow to a certain height and then suddenly develop some unsightly eccentricity. You will see it often in humans. I have a theory that the individual represents in his development the whole procession of his ancestors, and that such a sudden turn to good or evil stands for some strong influence which came into the line of his pedigree. The person becomes, as it were, the epitome of the history of his own family.

A. Conan Doyle, 'The Empty House'
The Return of Sherlock Holmes

An object created by the human mind, that is to say a significant object, is 'significant' for the very reason that it points beyond itself, that it is the expression and exponent of a more general intellectual truth, of a whole world of feeling and ideas, a world which has found in it its more or less perfect symbol. We measure the degree of its significance by the success of its symbolic representation. What is more, the love of such an object is also significant in its own right. It says something about the person who experiences this love.

The Magic Mountain (III, 904)

Contents

	Acknowledgements	*page*	xi
	Chronology		xii
	Chronology of Buddenbrooks		xxi
1	Life and works		1
2	Retrospect on the nineteenth century		10
3	The evolution of the novel		20
4	The theme of decline		29
5	Stages in decline		38
6	Thomas Buddenbrook		56
7	Narrative technique		69
	Point of view		69
	'Leitmotiv'		78
	'Bilse and I'		80
	Summary		83
8	The Buddenbrooks' decline: a typical story?		86
9	Literary background and reading public		94
10	*Buddenbrooks* and the 'crisis of the novel'		104
	Suggestions for further reading		113

Acknowledgements

It is a pleasure to record my gratitude to those who have helped me during my work on this book, and especially to Peter Stern, from whose inspiring teaching and scholarship my own interests in Thomas Mann first developed and who has guided the volume to its present form with the clear-headedness and unfailing kindness that have enriched German studies for so many colleagues and past pupils. Jochen Vogt generously gave me access to the materials he had collected for his own outstanding study of *Buddenbrooks*, and for this and the privilege of working with him in various projects in the field of modern German literature, I would like to record my thanks. Christian Oeser with characteristic generosity read my early drafts, and Helen Gallagher brought them, if not me, into the electronic age and the word-processor. To them all, as to the German Academic Exchange Service, *fons et origio* of so much work in German, I owe sincere thanks. To whom else could I dedicate this book about Mann's great family novel, however, than to my sons?

Note on editions used

References to the text of *Buddenbrooks* are given in the form of part and chapter numbers (e.g. 2, 4). References to other works by Mann are taken from the standard 13 volume edition (*Gesammelte Werke in dreizehn Bänden*, 2nd edition, Fischer, Frankfurt am Main, 1974) and given in the form of volume number (roman) and page number (arabic): e.g. III, 904. Other references are to works listed in the short bibliography. Translations from the German texts are in all cases my own. This is not to challenge the standard English translation of the text by Helen Lowe-Porter, available in the UK (Secker & Warburg and Penguin Books) and in America (Alfred Knopf). I was not concerned with producing a reading-text, but with conveying precise meaning.

Chronology

	Thomas Mann's life and work	Relevant literary events	Important historical events
1794	Johann Siegmund Mann made a citizen of Lübeck.		
1806			Overwhelming defeat of Prussian troops at Jena. Continental blockade. French troops in Lübeck.
1813			Lübeck freed by troops under Crown Prince Bernadotte. Battle of Nations signals final phase of Napoleonic era.
1815			Congress of Vienna. Lübeck confirmed as member of German Confederation and as a Free City.
1820			Final Acts of Congress establish Metternich system in central Germany.
1830			July Revolution in Paris. Bourbons replace Orleans. Echoes in Germany soon suppressed.
1832			Major public expressions of liberal nationalism variously suppressed (1832 Hambacher Fest, 1835 Young Germany, 1837 Göttingen Professors).
1833			Foundation of Customs Union (Zollverein) without Austria.

1837	Marriage of T.M.'s grandfather, Johann Siegmund Mann jun. (1797–1863), to Elisabeth Marthy (1811–90).	Accession of Louis-Philippe in Paris, Rhine crisis. Early industrialisation (Borsig's first locomotive).
1838	Birth of daughter, Marie Elisabeth Mann.	
1840	Birth of Thomas Johann Heinrich Mann.	
1842	(Marie) Elisabeth Mann to boarding-school of Therese Boußet.	
1844		Weavers' unrest in Silesia.
1847		Despite Danish obstruction, Lübeck linked to Berlin–Hamburg railway at Büchen. Foundation of transatlantic HAPAG line in Hamburg.
1848		February revolution in Paris, March revolutions in Berlin, Munich and Vienna. German National Assembly in Paulskirche Frankfurt until 1849. In Lübeck a new constitution dissolves the distinction between citizens and inhabitants (formerly based on property rights). Universal suffrage, Senate elected by the lower chamber ('Bürgerschaft').
1849		Popular uprisings throughout Germany; defeat of the revolution.
1855		G. Freytag, *Soll und Haben*.

Year	Mann family	Literature	History
1856	Marriage of Elisabeth Mann to Ernst Elfedlt.	G. Flaubert, *Madame Bovary*.	
1857			Industrial expansion in Germany. Foundation of Norddeutscher Lloyd Bremen, followed by Bayer (Leverkusen 1863), BASF (Ludwigshafen 1865) and AGFA (Berlin 1873).
1859	Thomas Johann Heinrich Mann to Amsterdam.		
1862		I. Turgenev, *Fathers and Sons*.	
1863	Thomas Johann Heinrich Mann takes over the firm 'Johann Siegmund Mann, Corn Merchants, Commission and Transport Agents'.		
1864		E. and J. de Goncourt, *Renée Mauperin*.	Schleswig-Holstein War. Prussian and Austria vs. Denmark.
1866	Marriage of Elisabeth Mann to Albert Haag (daughter Alice b. 1867 and son Henry b. ?1870/1).		Austrian War. Prussia and Italy vs. Austria, Bavaria and Würtemberg. Lübeck introduces measures ending the monopoly of the guilds.
1867			North German Confederation founded under Prussian domination.
1869	Marriage of Thomas Johann Heinrich. Mann to Julia da Silva-Bruhns (1851–1923).		
1870			Franco–Prussian War.
1871	Birth of Luiz Heinrich Mann (d. 1950).	F. Nietzsche, *The Birth of Tragedy*.	German Empire proclaimed. Kaiser Wilhelm I, Chancellor Bismarck.

1875	Birth of Paul Thomas Mann.		Lübeck's constitution amalgamated with that of the German Empire.
1876		R. Wagner inaugurates the Bayreuth festival.	
1877	Birth of Julia Elisabeth Theresa Mann. Thomas Johann Heinrich Mann elected to Senate.		
1878			Laws against the socialists.
1880		E. Zola, *Le Roman expérimental.*	
1881	Move to new house, Beckergrube 52. Birth of Carla Augusta Olra Mann.		
1882	T.M. begins schooling.		
1883			
1884		A. Kielland, *Poison.* J. Lie, *Ein Malstrom.*	Germany begins to found colonial empire.
1885		A. Kielland, *Schiffer Worse* H. Ibsen, *The Wild Duck.* F. Nietzsche, *Beyond Good and Evil.*	Berlin reaches population of one million.
1886		P. Bourget, *Le Disciple.*	
1889	T.M. to Katharinum. Real-gymnasiale Abteilung. (Autumn) Mention of early dramas, a romance and lyric.		
1890	Birth of Karl Viktor Mann (April), centenary of firm (May), death of Elisabeth Marthy (December).		Lübeck's population 63,000. Bismarck dismissed as Chancellor by Wilhelm II.

1891	Thomas Johann Heinrich Mann dies of blood-poisoning.	H. Bahr, *Die Überwindung des Naturalismus*; F. Wedekind, *Spring's Awakening*.	
1892	T.M.'s mother to Munich. T.M. completes schooling.	G. Hauptmann, *The Weavers*.	
1893	(May) with Otto Grautoff edits *Der Frühlingssturm*. June/July: 'Vision'.	G. Hauptmann, *Hanneles Himmelfahrt*.	
1894	Enters insurance office in Munich. Occasional student at the Technical University. October: 'Gefallen' published.	H. Mann, *In einer Familie*.	
1895	First visit to Italy. May: 'Walter Weiler' (lost); June: starts work on *Das zwanzigste Jahrhundert*.	T. Fontane, *Effi Briest*.	Building of the Kiel Canal.
1896	To Rome and Palestrina. August/September: 'Der Wille zum Glück'; October: stories written in Italy (publication in brackets): 'Der kleine Herr Friedemann' (May 1897); 'Der Tod' (January 1897); 'Der Bajazzo' (September, 1897); 'Tobias Mindernickel' (January 1898); 'Luischen' (1900).		
1897	(Autumn): 'Bilderbuch für artige Kinder' (lost).		

1898	Work on *Simplicissimus*. Publication of *Der kleine Herr Friedemann*. Work on stories (publication dates in brackets): 'Der Kleiderschrank' (June 1899); 'Gerächt' (August 1899); 'Monolog' (1899); 'Der Weg zum Friedhof'.	
1899		H. Ibsen, *When We Dead Awaken*. Boer War.
1900	Military service curtailed through injury. Work on 'Tristan' (1903), 'Tonio Kröger' (February 1903) and 'Fiorenza' (August 1905).	H. Mann, *Im Schlaraffenland*; G. Frenssen, *Jörn Uhl*.
1901	October: *Buddenbrooks*.	F. Nietzsche, *Nietzsche contra Wagner*.
1902		A. Gide, *The Immoralist*. J. Conrad, *Heart of Darkness*.
1904		H. James, *The Golden Bowl*.
1905	Married Katja Pringsheim. Among their children are Erika (1905–69), Klaus (1906–49) and Golo (1909–).	
1906		J. Galsworthy, *The Man of Property*.
1909	*Royal Highness*.	
1910		E. M. Forster, *Howards End*.
1912	*Death in Venice*.	
1913		D. H. Lawrence, *Sons and Lovers*. M. Proust, *Swann's Way*.
1914	'Thoughts in time of war'.	Outbreak of First World War.

1916		J. Joyce, *Portrait of the Artist as a Young Man.*	
1918	*Reflections of an Unpolitical Man.*	H. Mann, Man of Straw.	Armistice, proclamation of Weimar Republic.
1922	Support for Weimar Republic declared in speech 'On the German Republic'.	T. S. Eliot, *The Waste Land.* J. Joyce, *Ulysses.*	
1923			Hitler's unsuccessful *putsch.*
1924	*The Magic Mountain.*		
1925		J. Dos Passos, *Manhattan Transfer;* V. Woolf, *Mrs Dalloway;* F. Kafka, *The Trial.*	
1926	'Lübeck als geistige Lebensform'.	A. Gide, *The Counterfeiters.* H. Hesse, *Steppenwolf.*	
1927			
1929	Nobel Prize for Literature.	A. Döblin, *Berlin Alexanderplatz.*	Wall Street Crash.
1930		R. Musil, *The Man without Qualities*	Beginning of final crisis of Weimar Republic. Chancellor Brüning governs via Emergency Decrees.
1932	'Goethe as representative of the age of the bourgeoisie'.		
1933	February 11 Leaves Germany in fact for exile. First volume of *Joseph and his brothers* appears. Further volumes in 1934, 1936 and 1943.		January 30. Hitler appointed Chancellor.
1934	First visit to USA on invitation of publisher Alfred Knopf.		

1935	Honorary doctor of Harvard. Meeting with President Roosevelt. Erika Mann marries W. H. Auden in order to obtain UK citizenship.		
1936	Loss of German citizenship.	K. Mann, *Mephisto*.	
1939	*Lotte in Weimar*.		World War and 'Final Solution'.
1940	Start of BBC broadcasts to Germany.		
1941			
1947	*Doctor Faustus*.	B. Brecht, *Mother Courage*.	
1948		B. Brecht, *The Caucasian Chalk Circle*.	Following currency reform in Western occupation zones of Germany Berlin Blockade.
1949			Foundation of Federal Republic of Germany and German Democratic Republic. Adenauer first Chancellor of FRG.
1950			Korean War encourages industrial revitalisation of Federal Republic.
1951	*The Holy Sinner*.		
1952	Returns to Europe. Residence in Switzerland.		
1953			Death of Stalin.
1954	*Confessions of Felix Krull*.	M. Frisch, *Stiller*.	
1955	August 12. Death.		Federal Republic enters NATO.

Chronology of *Buddenbrooks*

Part One	Celebration of Meng Straße house	October 1835
	Tom aged 9, Tony 8, Christian 7	
Part Two	Birth of Clara	1838
	Deaths of Antoinette and	
	Johann Buddenbrook	1842
	Tom enters firm; Tony to Weichbrodt's school	
Part Three	Tony − Grünlich	1845
	Tom to Amsterdam	1846
Part Four	Christian to South America	
	'Revolution' in Lübeck and death of	
	Lebrecht Kröger	1848
	Grünlich bankruptcy	1850
	Death of the Consul	1855
Part Five	Death of Gotthold Buddenbrook	1856
	Christian returns from abroad	
	Marriages: Clara–Tibertius, Tom–Gerda	1856–7
Part Six	Tony–Permaneder. Christian to Hamburg	1857
Part Seven	Birth of Hanno	1861
	Tom elected Senator	1862
	New house in Fischergrube. Clara dies	1864
	Big losses as a result of Austro-Prussian War	1866
Part Eight	Christian returns	1867
	Centenary of firm	1868
	Weinschenk to prison	1871
Part Nine	Death of the Konsulin	
Part Ten	Hanno in Travemünde	1872
	Death of Thomas Buddenbrook	1875
Part Eleven	Christian marries Aline Puvogel	1876
	Day at school and death of	
	Hanno Buddenbrook	1877
	Gerda leaves Lübeck	

Chapter 1

Life and works

That *Buddenbrooks* is in many respects an autobiographical novel is irrelevant to the reading pleasure it affords. Thomas Buddenbrook is presented in so rounded and human a manner that, even if we did not know Mann's explanation that the figure is both a portrait of his father and a self-portrait, we could not mistake the special position which he occupies in the novel. The vitality and infectious exuberance of Tony Buddenbrook does not increase when we see the figure of Thomas Mann's aunt Elisabeth Haag-Mann as her model, nor is Hanno's viewpoint on the world more compelling for our knowledge that in so many respects it reproduces Mann's own childhood experiences. It requires in any case no profound scholarship to see the limitations to autobiography, since manifestly Thomas Mann did not die of typhus at the age of sixteen. The richness is in the novel, not in a biography behind the novel.

All the same, a writer's biography, in the broadest sense, is never irrelevant to an understanding of the literary work. The process by which experience is transformed into fiction shows the particular configuration of a writer's literary imagination, and if we see the writer's life as an expression of concrete historical possibilities and limitations in a given age his work takes on a further dimension as a creative exploration and redefining of those possibilities. Even so, some writers' biography will remain in the background, under stones which only literary historians will turn over, whereas for other writers, such as Thomas Mann, their own life has a foreground position; they find within themselves and the biography chance has decreed for them the material for a lifetime's work. Such writers notice this as a characteristic of themselves; they wonder at the health or usefulness of their own preoccupation with self, in which their opponents see merely a manifestation of privilege and material well-being; at all events such writers are driven to explore and justify not only the circumstances of their own biography, but their own preoccupation with it in their literary work. Such has been Mann's fate, and that of his first novel *Buddenbrooks*. Perhaps it is understandable that a writer, producing so mature a masterpiece at the age of twenty-five (many early reviewers of the novel spoke of their surprise at learning that its author was not, as aspects of its style and themes might suggest, well over sixty), should spend so much time reflecting on its origins and importance in his life, trying to persuade himself that it was his own product and not a cuckoo's egg laid in his nest.

Paul Thomas Mann – his schoolboy publications used the pseudonym Paul Thomas – was born on 6 June 1875 at number 36 Breite Strasse in the city of Lübeck, which lies close to the Baltic Sea some few miles west of the present Federal German border. His father, Thomas Johann Heinrich Mann (1840 – 91) had since 1863 been the owner of the family firm of commission agents and corn merchants. He had held the largely honorary position of Royal Netherlands Consul in the city, and since 1877 the far more prestigious elected office of Lübeck Senator. Thomas Mann's mother (1851 – 1923) had been born in Brazil, being christened Julia da Silva-Bruhns, but educated as a boarder in Lübeck. Her father was originally from the city and owned a plantation in Brazil, while her mother was of Brazilian nationality and Portuguese-Creole extraction. Julia da Silva-Bruhns was well-known for her beauty and musical talent, and in his fiction Mann ascribed artistic temperament to a strong polarity of inherited characteristics: seriousness and self-discipline on the father's side and a more passionate, frivolous and sensuous outlook on the mother's side.

Mann's childhood was a happy one, a group of five children in a spacious house, built by his father in 1881 on the Beckergrube 52, surrounded by the cultural and historical richness of a city proud of its traditions. Mann enjoyed the life of the city from the inside, son of one of its prosperous and respected families. His sisters, Julia and Clara, were younger than Thomas Mann; his brother Luiz Heinrich Mann (1871 – 1950), who was also to distinguish himself as a writer, although his work has been slower to be established in the literary canon of Western Europe, was four years Thomas's senior. Their brother Viktor was born in 1890.

Thomas Mann regarded his schooling as a distasteful and unprofitable episode. As *Buddenbrooks* makes clear – Part Eleven is among other things a savage attack on the ethos and methods of Mann's former school – the 'Realgymnasium' brought Mann neither intellectual satisfaction nor the skills necessary to a business career. He repeated a class twice, and left without the formal leaving certificate, the 'Abitur', thus joining the select group of German intellectuals (among them Albert Einstein) who showed lack of success at school to be no measure of intellectual distinction. Without the comradeship and intellectual excitement of a literary club to which he belonged, school days in Lübeck would have had nothing to offer Mann, save the painful demonstration of the hostility of the city and its 'culture' to the type of intellectual activity which interested him. From these years date Mann's earliest literary efforts: dramatic and lyrical poems whose titles have been preserved but whose texts are largely lost.

Very shortly after the family had enjoyed the pinnacle of its public success, the civic celebration in 1890 of the centenary of the family firm, Thomas Mann's life changed drastically. The death of his grandmother (it is her house opposite the Marienkirche which is preserved today as the Buddenbrooks' house) was followed by the unexpected and premature death of his father, on 13 October 1891. According to his testamentary instruction, the firm was liquidated. None of his children was permitted by the will to attempt to carry on the firm – not that they had wanted to, but the firm was certainly a good business proposition still. After a short period in Lübeck, Frau Julia Mann moved with the four younger children to Munich. Heinrich Mann was already attempting a literary career, and after Thomas had finished his schooling in Munich he was impatient to do the same. In March 1894 he left school and took up work in a fire insurance office, echoes of which can be found in his portrait of Hugo Weinschenk's downfall in *Buddenbrooks*. It was in the insurance office, 'among sniffing clerks', that Mann wrote what was to be his first published work, the short story 'Gefallen' (Fallen), which brought his name for the first time to the attention of literary circles in his new home.

Finding fire insurance as little fun as school, Mann gave up his job and determined upon a journalistic career. He registered as an occasional student at the Technical University of Munich, following 'from time to time regularly and not entirely without profit' lecture courses on economics, history, aesthetics and literature. Mann gradually became better known in the Munich literary scene, both as a writer of short stories and, for a brief period, as co-editor with his brother of the very reactionary journal, *Das zwanzigste Jahrhundert* (The Twentieth Century). With his brother he undertook extensive travels in Italy and it was while Mann was in Rome that 'Der kleine Herr Friedemann' was published, along with four other short stories, in the eponymous collection in 1898. This collection marked the sealing of Mann's life-long association with the influential publisher Samuel Fischer. The seeds of *Buddenbrooks* were sown in a remark of Fischer's early in 1897, to the effect that he would be interested to see a longer prose work from the young author's pen.

A long stay in Italy in the winter of 1897/8 was largely taken up with work on the novel, but when Thomas returned in April 1898, the uncompleted manuscript of *Buddenbrooks* in his luggage, he turned once more to journalism, obtaining a post on the editorial staff of the popular satirical magazine *Simplicissimus*. As all the editorial staff had just been arrested or gone abroad on a charge of lese-majesty, it was a good time to be looking for a job with the magazine. His editorial work distracted him from completing his novel, but it gave him still more contacts with the literary world of Munich and a stronger sense of the literary climate into which he was to launch his own works. *Buddenbrooks* was not his

only project, and several of his best-known stories originated
in this period, including 'Tonio Kröger' which was conceived
during a journey to Denmark via Lübeck in September 1899.
In May 1900 *Buddenbrooks* was completed and the
manuscript dispatched, and Mann enlisted for his one-year
compulsory military service. In December he was discharged
as medically unfit, an inflamed tendon making Thomas Mann
one of the less tragic victims of the German army's parade
march.

During his military service Mann received the first response
from Samuel Fischer to the manuscript he had submitted.
Fischer praised the novel, but asked that it be drastically
shortened. Although he would in later life speak ironically of
the length of his first novel, Mann replied with a passionate
defence of its length as one of its principal stylistic features,
and with exemplary confidence in his author Fischer agreed
to publish the novel with only superficial amendments. (The
pages which Mann rewrote from his original manuscript are
the only survivors of his handwritten copy of the work.) The
novel eventually appeared in October 1901 in two volumes. It
sold well, certainly better than *Der kleine Herr Friedemann*,
but its price kept sales to a modest level. The publication of
a cheap, one-volume edition in 1902 helped the novel to a
wide popularity. It remains Mann's major-selling novel and,
with 'Tonio Kröger', the most abidingly popular of all
Mann's works.

The role of the early stories in Mann's development is complex, reflecting his progress on two distinct though inter-
related levels. We may see these stories as part of an apprenticeship leading to the precocious mastery revealed in *Buddenbrooks*. Within few pages they deal with failure and
death, and with the phenomenon of the social outsider. Certain of their themes have no part in the novel − notably the
portrayal of the consequences of an often grotesquely
misplaced love − but other themes reappear in *Buddenbrooks*: such as the connection between sensitivity and
physical debility, which is such a strong theme in 'Der kleine
Herr Friedemann'. Particularly significant is the story 'Der

Bajazzo' (September 1897), an account of the decadent dilettante, a clear prototype for the figure of Christian Buddenbrook, although it is significant that the novel dispenses with the device of an unhappy love as the destructive force in this figure's life. In terms of style we see how sketchy impressionistic techniques of 'Vision' and 'Gefallen' give way to an increasing mastery of psychological narrative, which Mann came to see not as an interest in the abnormal, the melodramatic and the grotesque, but as an intellectual penetration of everyday reality. In a letter of 25 October 1898 to his friend Otto Grautoff, Mann explained that he had overcome his excessive enthusiasm for the 'Viennese "art"' and vanity' of Hermann Bahr, to whom his first published story 'Vision' (1893) had been dedicated. Although, as we shall see, he never lost his enthusiasm for Bahr's commitment to launch literature once again onto the paths of psychological investigation, Mann's interests had led him on the one hand to realism, and on the other to more socially-orientated psychological investigation.

The second level on which the short stories are important is as an apprenticeship, not so much in the techniques internal to literature, but in the function of literary creation within the process of shaping one's individual life. T. J. Reed has usefully pointed to a shift from the excessive literariness of the early stories, many of which do not attempt to articulate Mann's own experiences but simply re-work existing literary material which Mann had read. In the course of the stories — Reed sees 'Der Bajazzo' as an important turning-point — he acquired the confidence and ability to handle in fiction issues central to his own life. Mann himself regarded 'Der kleine Herr Friedemann' as the turning-point. In a revealing letter to Grautoff on 6 April 1897, he wrote: 'Since "Der kleine Herr Friedemann" I have suddenly become able to find the discreet forms and masks in which I can go into society with my experiences. Whereas previously, even I wanted to communicate only with myself, I needed a secret diary.'

This ability to express himself through the creation of separate and distinct fictional characters and to transcend mere literary games, was acquired in the short stories. They represent therefore more than exercises in literary technique. Indeed, Susanne Otto has suggested that they form part of Mann's socialisation, outlining trial drafts of possible actions, projecting fears and self-doubt about his life's future shape into literary models, testing out forms of social alienation, its possible overcoming and its cost. We see a continuation of these efforts, perhaps, in Mann's attempt to formulate a justification of his writing, an overall aesthetic, which does not break entirely with the values of the bourgeois world. Reflecting on *Buddenbrooks* in the revealing short essay, 'Bilse and I' (1905/6) — written to defend his novel against the claim that it merely records real people and events — Mann explicitly denied that aesthetic values meant a suspension of normal ethics. He saw the activity of an artist not as an alternative to bourgeois values (however much he might have felt exiled from the profession traditional to his family) but as the form in which he had to find ethical justification for his life. In other words, traditional ideas of the work ethic were important even within the alternative life style of the artist. In 1918 Mann commented revealingly

In truth, 'art' is only a means to fulfil my life ethically. My 'œuvre', if you will pardon the phrase, is not the product, purpose or aim of an ascetic-orgiastic denial of life, but an ethical expression of my life itself. This is shown by my tendency to autobiography, which is ethical in origin but certainly does not exclude the most lively aesthetic will to objectivity [Sachlichkeit], distancing and objectivising [Objektivierung].   (XII,105)

This remark shows that Mann's undertaking in *Buddenbrooks* was an exploration of self which would not be self-indulgent, and which would, by the rigour of its self-examination and the labour of its craftsmanship, be justified in society. Behind the polished construction of the novel we should not miss the personal quest involved in the novel's double mission: being both the attempt to draw up an inventory of the inheritance Lübeck left to its recalcitrant son, and a testing of his standpoint as outsider-turned-critic. It is a sign of the personal and artistic maturity of the work that such personal enquiries are carried out through fictional characters presented with exemplary detachment.

In view of these considerations, reaching beyond literary-historical matters of theme and style, it is clear that the relationship between *Buddenbrooks* and the remainder of Mann's works would be a special one. Whether we see the works before *Buddenbrooks* as a preparation for the thematic concerns of the long novel or as a working-out of the positions which enabled him to write his first major work, that first novel always had a special part in his *œuvre*. Mann himself often spoke of *Buddenbrooks* as a key to his later work – not simply in the general sense that, as a work concerned with his own background, it contains the themes and seeds of life's work to come, but more especially in relation to the works which immediately follow *Buddenbrooks* and which focus on the problems of the artistic life in society. The most famous of these are 'Tristan' (1903), 'Tonio Kröger' (1903) and 'Der Tod in Venedig' (Death in Venice) (1912). Mann summarised the relationship between his first novel and these shorter works when he referred to 'Tonio Kröger' as a 'prose ballad [. . .] played on the instrument which I had made for myself: the large novel' (XII,90), a phrase which neatly expresses the achievement of *Buddenbrooks* in creating a framework within which Mann could make his own experiences artistically productive, a scale of tone and theme on which other works might draw and to which they might add new elements.

Certainly one is justified in thinking of *Buddenbrooks* as the key-work for the period of Mann's writing which ended with the First World War, the period of his life of which *Betrachtungen eines Unpolitischen* (Reflections of an Unpolitical Man) (1918) provides an intellectual distillation, with its repeated exploration of the theme of 'Bürger-Künstler', art and life; and yet there is little doubt that Mann never shook off the Buddenbrooks world. If *Der Zauberberg* (The Magic Mountain) (1924) sees him preoccupied with themes drawn above all from the war years, it should not be forgotten that Hans Castorp, the novel's hero, owes his intellectual and

moral outlook to a Hanseatic background which he shares
with the Buddenbrooks. The Joseph novels, the first volume
of which appeared in 1933, the year Mann left Germany in
protest against National Socialism, cover new ground. *Lotte
in Weimar*, however, re-enters the historical milieu of the
German middle classes through its exploration of the world
of Goethe, that 'representative of the age of the bourgeoisie',
to quote the title of Mann's speech at the Goethe centenary
in 1932. Mann wrote, for instance, of his sense of affinity
with the buildings and houses of Goethe's childhood, as an
expression of his intellectual habitus in Frankfurt, like
Lübeck a Free City within the Empire. So it was perhaps less
than surprising that in his final major novel, *Doctor Faustus*
(1947), Mann should return to the gabled late-medieval world
of the German cities in recreating the childhood of his hero
Adrian Leverkühn. Many features of this novel, including the
encounter with the devil, have their origins in the years during
which *Buddenbrooks* took shape. When Mann confessed to
the ambition to write in *Doctor Faustus* 'nothing less than the
novel of my epoch', he was simply taking forward into a more
troubled age the project of his youth, and it testifies to the
consequentiality of Mann's work that this project should
have its origins in the world of the Buddenbrooks.

Chapter 2

Retrospect on the nineteenth century

Before we look at the way in which Mann's projected novel came to fruition, it is useful to sketch in the historical situations in which and about which Mann was writing.

The novel opens in 1835 with the Buddenbrooks celebrating their occupancy of the new house. It closes in 1877 with Hanno's death. The actual events from which Mann set out are of later date, since they move back in time from the experiences of the young and adolescent Thomas Mann in the 1890s. The centenary of the Mann family firm took place in 1890, not 1868 as in the novel, and the historical sources Mann used in fact take the action back into the 1820s. He therefore telescopes into forty-two years a rather longer period of family history, and is able to incorporate historical structure into the novel without an excess of historical narration.

By telescoping the action, Mann keeps events within the life of one character, Tony Buddenbrook, who acts as a kind of measuring-rod for the lapse of time and the shift of attitudes. At the same time — this was a technique he learned from the French realists — Mann kept each generation in touch with characteristic historical figures and movements. Johann Buddenbrook represents the Napoleonic period: not accidentally does the dinner discussion in Part One recount the guests' experiences of the great man and his age. His son, the Consul, who disapproves strongly of Napoleon I on moral grounds (1,5), epitomises the quieter values of the post-Napoleonic period. The years from 1830 to 1848 (the July Monarchy in France: in Germany the period is often referred to as 'Biedermeier') combined domestic peace, not to say stagnation, with stirrings of the progressive ideology which would emerge in the 1848 Revolution. The Consul is the man of this period. Thomas Buddenbrook, an admirer of Louis Napoleon, experiences the transition into the new German Empire. Hanno, who has played in the nursery during the wars which brought about German unification, experiences its unpleasant realities. Thus the story reaches out from its original basis in relating the personal and domestic history of one family, trading in Lübeck across these years, and integrates it into a wider tableau of class, city, and country.

Thomas Mann's novel therefore takes its reader through the main currents of nineteenth-century history, from Napoleon's conquest of the German states to Germany's days as a super-power at the end of the century. Johann Buddenbrook senior, despite the horror stories of the occupying French armies in Lübeck, clearly owed much of his wealth to the need of those armies for grain and stores. In the years immediately following the defeat of Napoleon, Germany remained divided into many separate and often hostile states, some of them large and powerful like Prussia, others tiny, no bigger than a small city. There was little general sense of German national identity, and among the educated classes French culture and even language were widely used, as we see in the opening chapters of *Buddenbrooks*. Lübeck in the north was cut off from German territory by Danish possession of Schleswig and Holstein. Prussia exercised authority in the north east, Austria in the south, and the period 1815 – 48 was one of oppression in the German states, as the absolutist rulers tried to keep at bay their dual enemies, liberalism and nationalism. 1848 marked a brief attempt by the liberal middle classes to wrest constitutional change from the monarchs, but after initial successes the revolution and the National Parliament which it established in Frankfurt lost their way. This was partly the result of a conflict between the aims of liberalism and nationalism, the impossibility of balancing the right to self-determination of the Poles and the cause of German nationalism in Eastern Europe. Partly, too, the liberals showed themselves unable to relate to the pressure for change initiated by the working classes of Germany, which formed the second phase to the revolutionary movements begun in

March 1848. Finally, the liberals placed too much faith in the
constitutional processes of political debate and neglected
issues of power, save where their own interests with regard to
the proletariat were threatened.

As the forces of reaction re-established themselves in the
German states, it became clear that the hope for German
unity lay with two already existing processes. In the first
place, the steady advance of economic modernisation in
Germany created better communications and closer ties
between separate states. Customs Unions were formed, and
their progress continued without significant check through
the periods of political regression. It had always been part of
the political armoury of German liberalism to argue for national unity on economic grounds (Consul Buddenbrook is a
man of his time when he supports these moves), but after
1848 economic life increasingly took on a surrogate function,
replacing rather than underpinning the political activity of a
bourgeoisie frightened off the political stage by the set-backs
of 1848. The second crucial factor in German unification was
the increasing ascendancy of Prussia within Germany, the
success Bismarck achieved as Prime Minister of Prussia from
1862 and subsequently as the first Chancellor of the German
Empire (1871) in assuring the territorial integrity of Germany,
defeating Denmark, Austria and finally France in a series of
wars leading up to unification in 1871. The first two are the
wars through which Hanno plays as a child, and which surge
over Lübeck and back again, leaving Thomas 20,000 thaler
the poorer (7,8). Under the new Empire, German economic
and military strength increased at a hectic pace, completing
the transformation of a state which, in the first half of the
nineteenth century, was by common consent at least fifty
years further back in its economic development than its European neighbours, and politically more backward still.

The effects of this 'backwardness' in Germany's development as a modern state have often been discussed by
historians. For our purposes, we may note that it led among
the German middle classes to a paradoxical situation in
which, precisely at the apex of Germany's military and

economic power, a large section of the population took refuge in a backward-looking cult of tradition and showed little interest in the values and social forms which had brought them prosperity and unity. It was symptomatic of a widespread feeling that traditional values were being cast aside for the questionable advantages of economic modernisation. At the same time, however, the Empire represented the culmination of the aspiration of German intellectuals throughout the century: a unified German national state. The groups which protested against change could not protest too loudly, because what they were experiencing was what they had wanted, and it was only logical that their disquiet rarely took on a direct political form as an explicit criticism of social or economic policy, but instead took refuge in ideology, in a combination of protest and defeatism, opposition and inwardness. The phenomenon of 'cultural pessimism' is as striking a feature of Germany in the late nineteenth century as the vulgar and aggressive militarism for which the state is more generally known, and whose symptoms (other than those manifested in Hanno's school) are strikingly absent from *Buddenbrooks*.

On this larger stage of history Lübeck played a relatively minor role. The great days of the city had been the late fourteenth century, when the Hanseatic League had exercised immense power in the Baltic and North Sea areas, but it had remained prosperous enough through the centuries to preserve a strong cultural identity and the politically advantageous status of a Free City. It had limited civil rights through centuries when other German states suffered under absolutist monarchs; indeed in 1848, when in other German states the cause had been constitutionalism, Lübeck could point to a constitution dating back to 1669 and wonder (as the Consul enquires of the rebellious Carl Smoets in the amusing scene in 4,7) what all the fuss was about. All this gave Lübeck a pride in its economic, political and social structures, a pride which clearly emerges at many points throughout the novel: for instance in the account of Thomas's election to the Senate (7,4), in the distribution of the honorary consular titles

relating to established trading-partners both within and outside the Hanseatic League (we notice that Thomas Buddenbrook's father has the office of Consul, since he represents
the interests of the Netherlands); and in the highly class-
conscious manner in which Thomas Buddenbrook conducts
his dealings with the landed aristocracy in Lübeck's
hinterland. Such were the manifestations of the special status
of Lübeck in the nineteenth century.

Gradually, however, in the second half of the century,
Lübeck's relationship to the rest of Germany underwent
significant changes. As a result of two distinct processes its
special status was modified and then devalued. In the first
place, following the removal of Danish sovereignty over
Schleswig-Holstein, Lübeck was able much more fully to participate in the economic boom inside Germany. Added to this
were constitutional changes which did away with restrictive
and archaic practices in the city's ancient constitution, ending
− very belatedly − the power of the guilds, and permitting a
great increase in population. Lübeck's special status came to
an end finally in 1875, four years after German unification.
At the same time, certain shifts in the economic geography of
Germany were working against the city's interests. The growing population of Berlin as capital of the Empire made Germany an importer, rather than exporter, of food, and the pro-
visioning of the capital tended to favour nearby Stettin as a
Baltic port rather than Lübeck − a matter of no small
significance to a corn-business like the Manns'/Budden-
brooks'. The increasing ascendancy of Hamburg in the
American and colonial trade (many overtones of the
centuries-old rivalry of Hamburg and Lübeck emerge from
the Consul's visit to the Grünlich household in Part Four)
further undermined Lübeck's sense of being the leading north
German city. The construction of the Kiel Canal (1895) set the
seal on this decline.

We should not think of the historical background to the
novel as if it were simply 'given' or static, like the backdrop
to an historical tableau, fulfilling a decorative function as a
still life or as local colour. The fact that major historical

events remain in the background, discussed by Thomas and his barber, or sketched in *en passant* by the narrator, does not mean that they have no role in the novel. The period was one of great historical change and cried out for interpretation and perspective. That history yields meaning in accordance with the needs of the reader of history, and that historical facts as such are dead and irrelevant, was a dictum of Nietzsche's with which Thomas Mann certainly concurred. Only the history that can be brought alive in the portrayal of the family and is related to Mann's thematic concerns is likely to have made its way into the novel.

The process of selection from historical material is complex. It is not just that, in writing the novel, Mann selected from history as carefully as from his family papers and therefore left out events − such as the great Hamburg fire of 1842, or (more surprisingly) Richard Wagner's visit to the city in 1873. Of course facts are left out, otherwise novels would be as long as history itself. What is important is that the selection of facts implies an interpretation of history, one which Mann either gained through study or which, as he later conceded, he might have taken over 'half unconsciously' from his own background (XII, 140). At all events, Mann's presentation of German history is dominated by the Lübeck perspective. Unlike Theodor Fontane, with whom he is often appropriately compared, Mann has nothing positive to say about the Prussian tradition and next to nothing about the events on the road to German unification. The Danish and Austrian Wars appear in the narrative, but are heavily muted and form little more than the ironic background to the nursery games of Hanno. (Readers of Günter Grass's *The Tin Drum* will find there echoes from this chapter (7,8)). It is clear that Mann felt these events to be only marginally relevant to the story he wanted to tell. At all events, the novel's action lies outside the main stream of Bismarckian power-politics, although this does not imply a parochial perspective on events or any contravention of historical realities. Mann is anything but uncritical of Lübeck, but his portrait of nineteenth-century Germany is rooted in Lübeck.

In his concern for historical interpretation, Mann was very much a product of his age. We should recall how hectic was the upsurge in historical writing at the end of the century. This affected not only diplomatic and political history (in the wake of the great names of German historical writing — Ranke, Treitschke and Mommsen), but still more importantly social and economic history. While Mann's Lübeck perspective made him less than susceptible to a Prussian view of German history, the experience of his family's economic decline opened his eyes to the major events taking place in the social and economic life of the country. Had Mann's family come from the sort of professional background shared by so many nineteenth-century writers (public service, law, medicine, teaching, the church), he might not have felt so closely the dramatic changes which were transforming Germany, for they took place precisely in the economic sector.

At the beginning of the century, trade was in the hands of individual family firms such as the Buddenbrooks. The family house was coextensive with the office and even with the storerooms and warehouses, and the head of the family ruled over both with equal authority. Family firm did not only mean that all the family were active in the firm: it meant also that many of the employees were part of the wider family circle and that even the suppliers were seen as part of a paternalistic structure, linked to the merchant both by economic advantage and by loyalty and tradition. Upon this world, whose attitudes are enshrined in the elder Buddenbrook, two principal changes broke in. Trade became less personal, the individual merchant saw in his firm less an expression of his value-system, and more a means of profit alone. For the early Buddenbrooks, following the pattern of a primitive stage of capital accumulation, wealth was tangible (sacks of grain in the storehouse) and personal, residing in dowries, houses the family inhabited and in healthy bank-balances, read out to the family at funerals and engagement ceremonies, and meticulously recorded by Mann. By the end of the century wealth was less tangible, capital accumulation a more volatile process, the growth of joint-stock companies and stockmarkets moved the emphasis from the commodity in the warehouse to the seemingly self-generating activities of money itself. The changes for the merchant were enormous. Not only did he move into the uncharted waters of financial crises and bank-collapses for which he had no explanation: the market took on a life of its own, requiring mental and moral facilities for which the old merchant class felt ill-equipped by tradition and ethos.

As Mann tried to place his own experiences in the wider context of his family and society and in addition to place family and society in a still wider historical context, he found himself tackling a central issue of his day, one which the newly emerging social sciences were beginning to confront. While Marx's attention lay more with the changes in industrial capitalism, a number of sociologists (Tönnies, Weber, Simmel and Sombart most notably) were exploring themes still closer to Mann's own experience. In particular their consideration of the relationship between the traditional forms of economic activity and the new spirit of the age − in Tönnies' terms the difference between 'Gemeinschaft' (community) and 'Gesellschaft' (society), for Sombart the difference between traditional and new capitalist, ('Bürger' and 'Bourgeois'), for Simmel that between personal culture and the 'philosophy of money' − shows with what attention the decline of traditional classes was studied towards the end of the nineteenth century. There is no need to argue that such discussions 'influenced' Mann (many of them could not have influenced *Buddenbrooks*, for they are subsequent to it), or that Mann was trying to put into fictional form ideas which he had encountered in the social sciences. We must, however, see the drive towards historical understanding of the present as one of the 'pressures of history' in Mann's own generation, and in his novel.

It may, in conclusion, be useful to underline the deliberateness with which Thomas Mann introduced historical perspective into his narrative. It is convenient to show this through a comparison of the finished novel with its family sources, in particular with the letter written to Mann by his sister Julia, which contained information on the aunt who would be the model for Tony Buddenbrook. Julia's letter tells how their aunt had fallen in love with an army officer; how her parents, disapproving of this liaison, had driven her into the first disastrous marriage. It is here that Mann substitutes the Morten episode (3,4–12), a section of the novel with unmistakable political overtones.

Morten is a standardised portrait of a politically committed student of the day. He proudly shows Tony the sash which marks him as a member of the 'Burschenschaften', the student associations whose historical role was to preserve the liberal and national ideal from the days of the Napoleonic liberation. '"We liberated Germany"', he tells Tony: a claim even she finds a little exaggerated (3,8). At the same time it is clear that the figure of the doctor (Morten is studying medicine), representing scientific method, freedom from tradition, and meditation between the classes, was part of the literary tradition of European realism (compare the figure of Bianchon in Balzac). Early sketches for the novel suggest that Morten was to have had the function of objective commentator on the family's decline, standing above events and at a sovereign distance from the central characters (Lehnert,67). Noticeably, however, Mann settled on a much more discreet and understated function for the character, and allowed him to fade rapidly from the novel.

The fact that Mann is not writing a political novel, and does not give Morten prominence outside his brief flirtation with Tony, should not mislead us into thinking that the Revolution too is a mere episode, or that the actual course of events in Lübeck in 1848 (which Mann records with considerable accuracy) have no further implications for the novel. Just as historians see 1848 as a pivotal point in German history, so Mann suggests within the novel a wide implication for the event. There is more than a hint that certain of the ideas of '48, notably those on the emancipation of women, relate directly to the situation which Tony experiences as her parents thrust upon her the repulsive Grünlich. Yet Tony is more than a victim of such attitudes. Mann's exposure of the narrowness of outlook in which Tony is confined is not personal, but directed at her whole class and upbringing. Her renunciation of Morten in favour of Grünlich, her choice in favour of tradition − the 'link in the chain' (3,13) − rather than innovation represented by new ideas and classes, is the Buddenbrooks' 1848 failure, their failure to link with the politically progressive elements of the middle classes; it slams the door on their alliance with the spirit of the age, and Tony's marital disaster drags the family down with her. After all, the Buddenbrooks were not prominent enough a family to insist so strongly on their social superiority to the professional middle classes. Their prosperity went back little further than war-profiteering in the Napoleonic period, and Morten's romantically coloured view of Tony (which she gladly makes her own) as 'a princess' (3,8) in no way corresponds to reality. Tony is pleased at the title as it corresponds once again to the 'feudal' (2,2) views of her Kröger grandparents, which she finds so attractive, but which repeatedly have dire consequences for her. In rejecting Morten she is following a historically fateful course, and in illustrating this in his plot − in contradiction of his sources − Mann is showing that 'history' is anything but background. It is one of the instruments of knowledge which his text will use.

Chapter 3

The evolution of the novel

Buddenbrooks is the product of a short span of years. The first page is dated October 1897, the last page was written in mid-July 1900. In contrast to the twelve years which *The Magic Mountain* took to write, the composition period of *Buddenbrooks* is both short and homogenous.

Even within these few years, however, Mann's intention for the novel passed through three distinct phases. While Mann himself felt, as we have seen, that he reached self-assurance in his use of the medium of narrative writing with the story 'Der kleine Herr Friedemann', and while it is evident that a remarkable number of Mann's first thoughts found their way into the final form of the novel (so that it is not helpful to think of *Buddenbrooks* changing its emphasis because of Mann's inexperience as a novelist), nevertheless Mann's intentions shifted during the writing of the novel, and with this shift of intention came also a shift in literary *genre*. This shift should not be misunderstood as a sign of Mann's personal uncertainty: rather it was the youthfulness or immaturity of the social novel in Germany that did not enable Mann to put his themes across within an established genre. This was an aspect of the novel in Germany on which many of the early reviewers of *Buddenbrooks* were agreed. We shall see later that Mann rejected many aspects of the popular German tradition in the novel, and despite the major achievements of Theodor Fontane (1819 – 98) within the field of the novel of polite society – known and appreciated by Mann as he worked on his own novel – Mann had to look outside the German tradition for literary models.

Fontane had not attempted the theme that was Mann's starting-point: to integrate the problematic situation and the experiences of the artist into the novel of good society. Some

fifty years after he had written the first page of his novel
Mann recalled: 'I well remember that initially only the figure
and experiences of the sensitive late-comer Hanno were
important to me [. . .], that which could be produced from
most recent memory, by poetic introspection' (XI,554).

The original intention was straightforward. The novel was
to work over elements of Mann's own experiences as the non-
conformer in the family tradition, the aesthete who had
departed from the spartan north and taken up residence in the
artistic south, and it would portray his environment only so
far as it related to these experiences, although in fact Christian
and Tony both figure in the earliest notes for the novel
his home town seemed distant and remote, 'essentially no
more than a dream' (X,15). Perhaps that dream included an
element of nostalgia, but it related to a society which Mann
had been pleased to leave and which had little cause to
remember him with affection or pride. Thus the story he
wanted to tell would include the kind of malicious and
satirical caricature Heinrich and Thomas had used in their
'Picture book for well-behaved children'. This adolescent sar-
casm – in the Mann circle it was known as 'gippern' – was
part of the intention behind the novel, it made of Lübeck 'a
dream, grotesque and venerable' (X,15), an object of both
derision and paradoxical respect to its recalcitrant son.

Even before the first page of the original manuscript was
written, however, the projected novel had begun to take on
a new dimension, prompted by Mann's wish to give the dream
concrete and tangible life, and to set his own experiences in
the historical context of the family tradition. In part, this
shift of emphasis was brought about by Mann's own
'bourgeois' sense that writing was justified not simply as a
preoccupation with self but as a coming-to-terms with a
'venerable' reality; in part, too, it resulted from a growing
interest in other members of his family, notably in Elisabeth
Haag-Mann, the model for Tony; but in part also it was a
legacy from his reading of the realists, with their passion
for documentation and detail. At all events, as Mann later
recalled, he determined to tell his story 'ab ovo' (from the

egg) (XI,554), to look at family documents going back to earlier generations, and to understand his family's experiences as a product and expression of their society. Since Mann was cut off from first-hand sources and, in view of his projected topic, had not even thought that he would need them, he turned to his family for help in collecting the information with which to fill out his narrative, to bring to life the milieu in which his own immediate experiences had been gathered, and to convey the reality of additional characters. His mother supplied many details; family papers and letters were used; his sister Julia sent him a twenty-eight page account of the life and character of the aunt who was to appear so prominently in the novel as Tony Buddenbrook; his cousin Marty sent information in reply to specific questions about the economic life of the city, some concerned with details – such as corn prices and the like – and some much more directly contributing to the novel's plot, as Marty gave his opinion as to the most common forms which the economic decline of a Lübeck firm might take.

Mann's use of these sources has many interesting features. At a stylistic level they show his skill in assimilating a variety of materials into a consistent and personal style (what in a letter to Adorno in 1945 Mann called 'höheres Abschreiben' ('a kind of superior copying'), casting in a personalised epic form incidental documentary material, finding psychological keys to illuminate sources which are much less differentiated. The novel shows Mann's great ability to refashion material, to bring to life experiences which he knew only at second hand. Recipes supplied by his mother are transformed into the lively dinner conversations of the guests in Part One; a cartoon from *Simplicissimus* comes to life as Herr Permaneder; memories of Goethe's *Werther* go into the Consul's enthusiasm for the family's neglected garden (1,5); and other words or images from Mann's reading give us Grünlich and his slimy name, and that mischievous 'x' which Hanno vainly hunts across his maths books. The novel is a patchwork, yet so superbly joined together that there is only one pattern. As we look at the sources, we notice too that Mann's awareness of his novel's thematic shape and direction was much stronger than his allegiance to mere historical chance in the narrative which his family skeletons bequeathed to him. He changed, as we saw, major features of Aunt Elisabeth's story to suit his own purposes: notably the Morten episode. Invented too is Tony Buddenbrook's return to Lübeck after her disastrous second marriage. Julia Mann's account had much to say of other colourful episodes in their aunt's life — her sadness when possible engagements to a Prussian lieutenant and to a South German nobleman were wrecked — but Mann ignored these. He was also highly selective in his approach to the reasons Marty had proffered for the decline of a Lübeck firm, and modified those which he decided to use. As he subsumed elements from Marty's purely economic account into the wider historical and psychological perspective of his novel, Thomas Mann revealed from the start that his focus would be radically different and that the causality he traced behind events would be far removed from that which his cousin suggested. If, as a child of his class and of his literary age, Mann was interested in documentary material, it was as grist to an artistic intention, not as providing the shaping principle of the work itself.

Already, however, one can see that there would be problems of organisation and perspective in combining Mann's original intention — the inward and subjective story of the late-comer aesthete — with the much less introspective story of the family's colourful fortunes and the background against which that story was played out. It was here that the question of genre — of what type of novel Mann wished to write — arose. Certain types of novel could handle the personal story; for the other elements a different form might be required. It is well known, for instance, that Mann greatly enjoyed the Scandinavian family novels of Kielland and Lie and read them intensively at the time of writing *Buddenbrooks*. They were appropriate models for certain aspects of Mann's intention in portraying family history, and sympathetic in their evocation of a common cultural milieu. Not for nothing was there a sense of cultural affinity across the Baltic, with Bergen merchants sending their children to be educated in Lübeck and creating honorary consuls among the Lübeck bourgeoisie. Kielland's *Poison* offered Mann a type of novel which combined, within a milieu very similar to Lübeck and with an intention not unrelated to Mann's, the study of a sensitive youth's rejection of school with a broad picture of the norms and life-style of the society. Nevertheless, for all their affinities, the Scandinavian writers lacked much that was important to Mann's novel from its very inception. The atmosphere of their work, damp with the sea-mists that swirled also round the gables of Lübeck, might be nostalgic, but it had nothing cosmopolitan to it. Perhaps it is that tendency towards parochialism which has left Kielland and Lie's work so short of an international following, especially in comparison with the public Mann's work reached. If it was parochial, their work also had nothing to say about the experience of art; it could hardly satisfy fully the needs of the conscious exile from Lübeck, who was deliberately savouring in Italy the joys of an aesthetic existence.

Not only did much of Mann's reading point in ways he did not wish to go: his sources themselves implied and, in the case of Julia's letter, openly expressed, ideological and moral values with which Mann was not necessarily in sympathy. Including them in his manuscript would bring the novel close to what Nietzsche had dubbed 'antiquarian history', a pious and reverent registering of the soil in which one's roots and origins can be traced, an attitude which is typified in the chronicle style of the Buddenbrooks' family papers, '[. . .] in which was expressed the discreet and therefore still more dignified respect of a family for itself, for tradition and history' (3,13).

Even quantitatively Mann's sources presented him with a problem. As new material flooded on to his desk, and as he found that 'egg' from which he and his family's story had emerged ever more elusive, so the novel's centre of gravity shifted further away from Hanno and the material came to resemble a civic chronicle, a history of the city of Lübeck across nearly one hundred years. This in turn made new demands on the novel's form, and, thanks to Mann's extensive reading of European literature during these years, he hit upon a form which could handle both the thematic needs and the sheer volume of his material. Of particular importance was his encounter in 1897–8 with a lesser-known novel of the Goncourt brothers, *Renée Mauperin* (1864).

The novel offered Mann two stylistic features which (with reinforcement from other realist writers) came to have a marked influence on *Buddenbrooks*. The use of short selective chapters (from Tolstoy, Mann took over the organisation of these chapters into separate parts) and a witty combination of links and breaks between the sections give the work a lightness in handling voluminous material. It is a stratagem which makes possible the celebrated opening of the novel with its unsituated, indeed somewhat mysterious dialogue. (*Renée Mauperin* begins with a conversation which we only gradually realise to be taking place between two people swimming in the Seine.) Secondly, Mann took from the Goncourts' novel the technique of associating the generations of a family with a particular historical period. There is nothing original about this technique: clearly Renée's father will tend to personify the Napoleonic France in which he spent his youth, and Renée's friends will in turn (like Morten Schwarzkopf) be shaped by the events of 1848. But, although nothing particularly subtle is implied by this method, it greatly helped Mann to relate family history to public history, and to find in the socio-historical placing of individual characters and events a distanced standpoint from which to view and portray his own family. The obvious affinities between the character of Renée and that of Tony Buddenbrook confirm the importance of the model.

The European realist movement did not merely offer Mann organisational principles for his voluminous subject-matter. It had developed into literary method precisely that type of critical intellectual enquiry into social behaviour which Mann needed to analyse his own experiences. Although in many ways he wished to go beyond realist themes and techniques (we see this in his approach to the theme of art, in his attitude to heredity and his use of psychology), and however attracted he had been, as we shall see, to those writers who claimed to have 'overcome' naturalism, realism offered Mann the ideal framework in which to 'objectivise' his life and to 'distance' himself from his society. We pointed to this process in our discussion of the novel's relationship to history: a still more telling example is in the approach of the novel towards a theme which greatly interested other realist writers — organised religion.

In the style of family chronicle, or the pious antiquarian history of a notable city, Mann's view of the Church as an institution might have been that of the local historian, keeping a ledger of the incumbents of the Marienkirche, a quaint character here, an admirable man of God there. Instead he chose to interpret the religious theme of the novel sociologically. His intention emerges in the contrast between the opening scene, rehearsing a catechism which causes an eight-year-old city girl to give thanks for the creation of her 'land and cattle' — an anachronism which amuses her grandfather with his Enlightenment scepticism — and the closing scene where it is left to the few scarred survivors of the family circle to proclaim their confidence in that catechism's teachings on the Hereafter. The opening and closing scenes locate the family's decline firmly within the history of ideas, in a period perched uncomfortably between confident rationalism, self-confident Protestantism and nihilism. Despite images which strikingly encapsulate a sceptical view of religion — Johann Buddenbrook's easy contempt for superstition, the pietistic excesses of the Jerusalem evenings, Hanno's mocking view of religion from the heights of the organ loft, or the reduction of religious education to head-counting among Job's sheep and camels — and despite the many reviewers of the novel who saw in it a deliberately anti-Christian work, Mann's intention is plain: to investigate the social and historical function of religion in his own family's history and in the history of his culture and class.

Quite evidently, Mann's interests focus on two themes: the relationship between religion and capitalism, and between religion and the family's decline. When Max Weber published his monumental work *The Protestant Ethic and the Spirit of Capitalism* in 1905 — a work treating a similar theme to R. H. Tawney's *Religion and the Rise of Capitalism* (1934) — Mann recognised the affinities with his own novel. He records the motto over the door of the Meng Strasse house, 'Dominus providebit' (The Lord will provide), out of a genuine historical interest in the processes by which Protestantism adapted to, and was itself adapted by, the economic activities of his own class. The family book with its beautifully observed combination of commercial handwriting and over-religious sentiments is a close record of this interrelation, as is the scrutiny of those telling phrases 'Christian, Father and Businessman' which Gotthold addresses to Johann (1,10), or that balance between piety and business sense with which Grünlich penetrates the family circle and which the Consul so astutely reverses when he extricates Tony from his clutches. One could not claim that Mann answers sociologists' questions — for instance, the chicken-and-egg question which Tawney reproaches Weber for not solving: namely whether the religion is the ideological form of capitalism, or capitalism the economic form of Protestantism — but there can be no doubt that Mann's eye is caught by socio-historical issues far more than by unproblematised local colour, or — still less — by confessional writing.

So it is that the actual clergymen who figure in the lives of the prominent Lübeck families are (with the colourful exception of the eccentric *habitués* of the Jerusalem evenings) characterised exclusively in terms of their function, and are as a result all-but interchangeable. Far from providing differentiated cameo-portraits of the local clergy, Mann merges the three generations of priests (Wunderlich, Kölling and Pringsheim) into a neat composite picture of a stable compromise between dogma and sensitivity to the needs of the rich. We see this clearly in Wunderlich's behaviour at the family celebration, and in Kölling's attitude towards Tony's marriage. As to the more personal questions of faith, Mann is content for the most part merely to show how the self-confidence and vitality of the Buddenbrook family is in inverse proportion to their need for religious consolation: a relationship highlighted early in the novel in the contrast between Johann and the Consul.

It was because of his adoption of realist techniques of this kind that Mann was able later to summarise the last two phases of *Buddenbrooks'* evolution by calling the work 'a municipal chronicle which had developed into a naturalist novel' (XII,115), claiming for it a place in German literary history as 'the first and only naturalist novel in Germany' (XII,89).

The question of literary classification need not concern us further at this moment. Mann had a strong tendency towards self-stylisation even in his allegedly non-fictional accounts of his life and works and presented as stages in the development of his work opinions which reviewers gave of the finished novel, so we need not feel his own comments necessarily to be binding. Whether the work is, or is not, a naturalist novel, will emerge only from close examination of the text. Nevertheless, Mann's account of the shift in intention and literary model which we have just followed is useful in drawing attention to a process characteristic of much that Mann would write. For in the shift from the 'story of a sensitive late-comer' through 'municipal chronicle' to 'naturalist novel' we are shown the way in which Mann based his work at its inception on autobiography, only then to interpret personal experience in terms of its representative status (representative here of a family, a city, perhaps a class), and then to intellectualise the representative function by subjecting not only the individual experiences but also the experience of the wider group critically to the devices − sociological, historical and ideology-critical − of the naturalist novel. Each of these stages represented for Mann major elements of his self-understanding as a writer, not simply in his first novel but throughout his life. It is true to say that Mann always remained faithful to this triadic structure, if not to the chronological sequence: autobiography, representation, analysis.

Chapter 4

The theme of decline

Some two years before the plan for *Buddenbrooks* had taken hold of him, Mann wrote to a friend a short sketch of his family's fall from grace, and the aspects of interest which the story contained for him:

My father was in business, a practical man but with an inclination towards art and interests outside the business. The eldest son (Heinrich) is a poet, but also a 'writer', with strong *intellectual* gifts, expert in criticism, in philosophy and politics. Then comes the second son (me), who is only an artist, only a poet, only a man of mood, without intellectual power, socially useless. Hardly surprising if finally the late arrival, the third son, devotes himself to the vaguest of the arts, the art furthest of all from the intellect, the art that requires nothing more than nerves and senses, and no brains at all – that is, music. That's what you call degeneration. But I find it devilishly nice. But, quite apart from that, with the impressions and influences he grows up amidst, the lad will scarcely develop into a *business man*.   (To Grautoff, late May 1895)

This letter, with its disarming openness, shows the charm which Thomas Mann found in the story of the 'sensitive late-comer'. It shows the stylisation of his family story, and it suggests that degeneration was a standard topos of intellectual discussion in his day. It makes obvious that the novel would have a descending structure. An early suggestion for a title for *Buddenbrooks* was 'Abwärts' (Downhill).

The finished novel lives up to this plan more strongly perhaps than to any other element in its preliminary drafts. Its sub-title, 'Verfall einer Familie' (Decline of a Family), gives the work its structure. From the opening scene of prosperity, in which three generations are assembled, to the final scene in which the remnants of the family mourn Hanno's death, the driving force of the novel is not merely that strong sense of the inexorable and natural movement of time passing through the generations, but an underlying pattern of decline, announced, happening and echoing after the event. A brief review of the individual parts of the novel will show how insistently the novel focuses on the descending line.

Part One offers an 'overture' (Vogt) to the novel, in the shape of a large family celebration in 1835, the first major dinner-party in the Buddenbrooks' Meng Strasse house. While a strong impression is given of wealth and success, Mann carefully introduces some factors which will delimit the latter: questions about the succeeding generation, family tension and disunities, and more generally the sad fact that they celebrate in the house of a family recently reduced to ruin. Part Two looks briefly at the potential for the future represented by the Consul and his children, Thomas, Christian and Antonie (Tony), and offers a contrast between its summary of Tony's 'happy childhood' and the immediate arrival in Part Three of a significant cloud on her horizon, the repulsive and dishonest suitor Grünlich. With Tony's engagement to Grünlich, recorded in the family book of whose sanctimonious tones we were previously given reason to be suspicious, and Thomas's surreptitious farewell to Anna, the petty bourgeois lover of his youth – both actions portrayed as fateful steps out of the protected world of childhood – Part Three concludes. Part Four moves from one catastrophe to the next, interweaving Tony's divorce with two highly dramatic deaths, not only that of Lebrecht Kröger, who represents the historical order which is just passing, but also the Consul's death, the principal figure of the whole of Part Four. Of all the deaths, so prominent in the novel, the Consul's enjoys the most obvious narrative attention: a set-piece natural description, recognised by critics and author alike as a show-stopper and allowed briefly to reverberate again in the hail-storm that later destroys Thomas's business hopes (8,5). Part Five brings the reader up to date with the downward progress of Christian, shows the life of the Konsulin and her daughter in a world of dubious and morbid piety, and introduces Gerda Arnoldsen into the family, 'the mother of future Buddenbrooks' (5,9), juxtaposing her in a consciously

dramatised way with the traditional world of the Buddenbrooks into which she intrudes, and strikingly ignoring details
of the honeymoon or of Gerda and Thomas's actual relationship. Within the range of the family novel it would be hard
to imagine a more portentous introduction. Part Six deals at
surprising length with Tony's calamitous second marriage,
counterpointed with Thomas's fear that his own marriage will
remain childless; the obviously comic elements in Tony's
story are held in check by the recognition that calamity is now
ushered in not by deception and swindling but by an event
whose triviality is emphasised by the narrator's playful
refusal to reveal it: the harmless insult of a man in his cups.
Over such trifles the family now stumbles. The good news
with which Part Seven opens (Hanno's birth and christening)
is immediately juxtaposed to Christian's obvious and grotesque inadequacies, just as Thomas's victory in the Senate elec-
tions is balanced by the death of his younger sister Clara. This
death not only undermines the family's morale, it is followed
by the unexpected news of a major business loss, another
drain on the capital sum which the head of the family, watch-
ed by the reader, keeps an anxious eye upon throughout the
novel, and whose diminution matches the family's more
general decline. Part Eight takes its shape from the ending in
scandal and disgrace of Tony's surrogate third marriage (for
that is the perspective from which her daughter's marriage is
shown), which acts as a pendant to the major business
disasters that strike Thomas. Part Nine is packed with
disaster, beginning with the Konsulin's death, describing a
major row between Thomas and Christian, culminating in the
sale of the Konsulin's home to Buddenbrooks' business
rivals, the Hagenströms, and ending − as an ironic counterpoint to the assurance of her happy childhood which conclud-
ed Part Two − with Tony's tears. Part Ten belongs almost
exclusively to Thomas and the final stages of his decline, and
ends with his only son Hanno screwing up his face against the
hard and cold wind that blows over the fresh earth of his
father's grave, that same wind which whistled round the
gables of the prosperous house at the end of Part One. The

final section belongs as exclusively to Hanno, to his confrontation with reality (represented by his school) and its ending in failure and death. At the end only his widowed mother, his aunt Tony and various harpy-like figures of the Buddenbrook sisters are left to mourn and to disperse.

Even if we did not know that the novel was written, so to speak, backwards, starting from the most recent events and gradually moving back to the more remote period of family history, we would certainly be struck by the increasing focus on the inner psychological dimension of its characters. Part Ten, for instance, is longer than Parts One and Two together. While we pass over Gotthold's marriage, the 1848 Revolution, the Consul's death, in a very few pages, we spend at least fifty pages with Hanno on that famous day at school and at the harmonium. In tracing the decline of the family, therefore, Mann not only covers a wide range of themes in his search for understanding: his enquiry turns towards an exploration of the hidden recesses of the soul.

Mann found in his reading of the family novels of Kielland and Lie no shortage of examples of decline. Like the Buddenbrooks, the heroes of these novels are often striving to maintain a family firm against a multiplicity of assailants. These assailants are, in fact, neatly personified among the minor characters of Mann's novel: drink and gambling, speculative greed or laziness in the conduct of the business, a crooked or criminal nature (the fascination with degeneration into crime and depravity was one of the more infectious by-products of naturalism's concern with heredity, as our opening quotation from Sherlock Holmes suggested), the pursuit of adultery or an unfortunate marriage. As we look at the 'suitors', the loose-living men in Lübeck society such as Gieseke and Döllmann. or again, as we read of the senility of Senator Möllendorpf, who dies with his mouth stuffed full of cake, we may see in these figures examples of the kind of open degeneration with which Kielland and Lie brought their families to their ruin. If it is evident where Mann drew on these devices, it is also evident that he uses them to illustrate rather than initiate decline (the Konsulin's somewhat

degrading, but financially by no means disastrous, entangle-
ment in the Jerusalem evenings − modelled on Kielland's
portrayal of the Haugianer sect in *Schiffer Worse* − is a case
in point); indeed, Mann gives these factors no role in
motivating the downfall of his principal family. Perhaps it
was in order to avoid such cheap foreshortenings of decline
that he attached so much importance to the length and
slowness of his narrative.

This can be seen even in the figure of Christian. Far from
being the cause of the family's decline (the material losses he
brings upon the family are little more than pin-pricks), Christian has the function of showing up in exaggerated form
characteristics more widely found in the family. In particular
he shows how his father (whom he so closely resembles) bequeathed to the family attitudes which degenerate into a total
inadequacy for life. It is precisely Christian's excessive imagination, his unwillingness to confront emotion (for instance
at his father's grave (5,2)), and the refusal to be truthful with
himself that cause Christian to be so useless in the business
world; but these characteristics, as the novel repeatedly emphasises, are inherited and shared with other members of the
family, in whom, in a less grotesque form, these general traits
contribute substantially to the decline of the family. Christian's argument with Thomas after their mother's death (9,2)
(which we shall discuss in detail in the following chapter)
makes clear Christian's function in the novel. It is worth
noticing also that the grotesque elements in Christian which
Mann plays down are those which have their origin in literary
models, in that fashionable concern of the 1890s for the dilettante and the decadent.

Mann's insistence that decay comes from within, not from
outside the family, is illustrated by an examination of his
treatment of marriage. The novel repeatedly emphasises the
continuity of the Buddenbrooks' marriages, and shows
decline to lie within a tradition, rather than in deviation from
it. In his marriage, Old Johann sets a model which subsequent
generations will follow. His first marriage, noted in the
family chronicle as 'the happiest year of my life' (2,1), had

ended tragically, but his choice of second wife is made pragmatically. He lives without passionate attachment to her, 'respectfully and attentively' (2,1): she has brought money into the family, and the marriage is successful, Johann being content to accept its emotional limits. As he records in the family chronicle: 'I could say much, were I minded to reveal my passions. However . . .' It is characteristic of the novel that it is the Consul who stops us reading more at that point, for his eye passes on from this part of the family book. It is this trait that he bequeaths to Christian, the unwillingness to know the truth, his disinclination to identify and name feelings. Perhaps the Consul is less confident in himself for having followed his father's example (and obeyed his hints) in marrying the wealthy Kröger daughter. It had hardly been a love marriage, but it too had been successful on the surface, producing prosperity and heirs. Only in the next generation does the system fail to work in practice as well as in the hidden depths of the soul. Tony does not follow her heart, but − like the Consul − obeys her father and the family tradition of which his choice is part: but it all leads to disaster, on which her father reproaches himself. Thomas too, although making a highly individual choice, follows the family tradition, as is shown in his reluctance to be clear about the relationship between love and money in *his* choice. He tells his parents that he is 'certainly not minded to go deep enough into myself to discover whether and to what extent my enthusiasm for Gerda has been increased by the large dowry' (5,7), thus exactly echoing his father's refusal to get involved with Johann's emotional uncertainties. Gerda's failure to produce more than one sickly child effectively ends the family; but the decline of the family, reflected in its marriages, is no biological accident. It involves an historical enquiry as to the reasons why the old and successful system of arranged, financially beneficial marriages no longer functions. Once more it is the norm which is under scrutiny, not the breaker of norms. It involves also the evolution in Thomas, as we shall see, of feelings not merely imperfectly attuned to the dual needs of the family (progeny and money), but also impatient for what is out of the ordinary, for the unusual and even the decadent. Tradition runs dry and the heart follows stranger and more disruptive paths. Such a study of decline has a logic which makes Kielland and Lie in comparison seem merely to deal out coincidences in their plot-constructions.

It is, of course, Tony's marriages which most prominently display the Buddenbrooks' inability to continue their success and prestige. Her capacity to bring disaster upon the family stems from no rebelliousness, however, but from excessive and unchanging loyalty to the family's no longer effective code of practice. Through all her misfortunes (perhaps even because of them) Tony manages to experience 'the feeling of personal importance'. This feeling gave her confidence in snubbing members of Lübeck's rival families, Julie and Hermann Hagenström especially. She married Grünlich to put them in their place, and Permaneder for the same reason, as is made explicit in her meeting with the Hagenströms during the outing on which she accepts Permaneder's proposal (6,6). As schoolgirl, wife, divorcee, mother-in-law and bereaved daughter and sister, from start to finish of the novel, she is driven by a sense of her own importance which she derives from the one source: the family. This process, subtly though it is observed, is simple and unchanging. Like Theodor Fontane's Effi Briest, she assents to her own nature, holds no surprises for the reader, who is moved by her predictability and the inevitable malfunctioning of the values she inherits rather than by surprising or unknown features of a more complex character. Her repeated insistence on traditional values, especially that sense of the 'vornehm' (7,1; 9,6 etc.), the *comme il faut* of her class, rings throughout the novel as nails driven into the family coffin.

It is clear from an early note on the novel that, at one point in its evolution, Mann had intended, perhaps in keeping with elements of naturalist theory, to stress the decline of the family as a biologically conditioned process, fatalistically accepted by the family members:

The strongly developed sense of family almost cancels out free will and self-determination, and leads to fatalism. Antonie says: I

inherited my taste for luxury from my mother, who in turn inherited
it from her family. She cannot do anything about it. She accepts the
features of her character without trying to correct them. That's how
I am. That's how I was bound to become. (Notebooks, Lehnert, 65)

Although we recognise Tony clearly in this early draft – in
fact, its elements are picked up into a scene immediately
preceding Grünlich's bankruptcy (4,6) – the note of fatalism
and passive acceptance increasingly fades from Mann's
presentation of Tony's character, and indeed it is only referred to in the novel at the point where fatalism is part of
Tony's confident assertion of her right, as a Buddenbrook, to
success and prestige. Fatalism as an acceptance of decline is
never part of her character. Mann's interest lies with those,
like Thomas, who try to combat the family's decline, whose
moral sense resists the blandishments of surrender to
decadence, who are determined not to give in to the erosion
of energy and health. And here Tony, albeit in an ambiguous
way, has a role to play at which the early note did not hint.
Despite the fact that the narrator draws comedy from her ill-
fortune and enjoys her solecisms, Mann insisted that Tony
was a positive character when the critic Kurt Martens attack-
ed the novel for its coldness (we shall see how a more sympathetic critic, Lublinski, answered such criticism). She was,
Mann claimed, when all is said and done, proud of her life
despite its disasters, and therefore proof that the novel was
not merely negative. Tony shares with Renée Mauperin the
pertness which always bounces back, the ability to start afresh
despite disasters, 'to adapt to each situation in life with talent,
skill and a lively pleasure in what is new' (4,10), and always
to resist the symptoms, if not the cause, of the family's
decline. But we are entitled to ask if her resistance contains
much in the way of positive values, whether anything lies
behind it other than a mere determination to survive. Tony's
constant objects of hatred – the Hagenströms, Catholicism,
Munich, yellow side-whiskers – perhaps merely disguise the
fantasy nature in her idea of the family, its increasing concern with the externals of status rather than with the
substance. The narrator's ironic detachment from the figure

does not make it easy to identify her with any other set of values. In a revealing comment, watching Tony's gusto in the role of mourner, the narrator speculates: 'God only knew how much pain and religious feeling and, on the other hand, how much of the self-complaisance of a pretty woman were contained in this expressive pose' (5,2). The narrator's refusal to comment decisively here is typical of the attitude towards Tony throughout: affection mingles with distanced enjoyment of the figure, admiration with scepticism. Nevertheless, it is clear that the fact of resistance represents a positive feature in the novel, and that the fatalism to which the Notebooks refer (and which has much in common with naturalist stereotypes) plays a smaller role in the novel than the dominance of the theme of decline might suggest.

Chapter 5

Stages in decline

The family's decline is placed in sharpest focus by a series of scenes in which, with diminishing success, the head of the family has to ward off threats to family interests. These scenes, consciously linked by the narrator, involve each of the first three generations. The series begins with the rejection of Gotthold Buddenbrook's demands for money. Gotthold, Johann's son by his first marriage and therefore the Consul's half-brother, has disgraced the family's sense of social prestige by marrying a shop-keeper and wishes to add injury by claiming a share of the family's increased fortune (1,10). The Consul and his daughter Tony enact the next crisis, just before a meeting to wind up the affairs of her bankrupt husband Grünlich, in which the Consul must decide between an obligation to keep the family together and the more tangible obligation not to throw good money after bad (4,7). Next it is Thomas who tries to cope with his mother's excessive generosity in parting with Clara's inheritance rather than keeping it within the family (7,7). Shortly afterwards he confronts Tony as she suggests a questionable business proposition (8,2 − 4). Finally, in the most heated and dramatic confrontation of all, Thomas and Christian test their conflicting strengths of purpose and their obligations to the family name. The occasion for this conflict is more trivial than any that have gone before − a few soup-plates and a canteen of silver − but the conflict is in deadly earnest and its outcome of crucial importance to the conclusion of the novel.

It is characteristic of the first of this series, Johann's discussion with the Consul, that it should take place late at night. It is an afterthought to the successful day, although the chapter is no afterthought to Part One. Clearly the scene is more significant to the novelist than the discussion is to

Johann. Johann will not discuss the issue Gotthold has raised
except to belittle his claims on him as father, businessman and
Christian. Family claims are clear to him: Gotthold should
have married into a wealthy family and brought capital into
the family. The business aspect is clear too: it is neither a legal
obligation nor sound business practice to pull money out of
his own firm and give it to Gotthold. Religious arguments
have no conflicting claims to make on Johann, and he
dismisses Gotthold's appeal to such obligations as
hyprocritical.

The Consul, however, who has brought this matter to his
father's attention, is troubled by his conscience. Ideas of
family harmony are less easily defined for him than for his
father. He has been reflecting, even during the celebrations of
the Buddenbrooks' move into their new house, on the
'destiny' which had fulfilled itself in the decline of the once
prosperous Ratenkamp family, into whose house the Buddenbrooks have just moved. Such a destiny, he fears, could work
through the family division, turning it, like the crack in the
wall of the House of Usher, into a 'heimlicher Riß' (a hidden
break) which will bring the whole edifice tumbling down. His
father is contemptuous of such ideas and of the mind that can
entertain them, although he is forced to acknowledge the
business success which his elder son's flexible and imaginative
brain can engineer. But the Consul's thoughts pass, and in a
rapid switch of mood his normal business-thinking, his clarity
and decisiveness, are reasserted. The calculating machine of
his mind whirrs and without further ado the answer pops out:
refuse Gotthold's demands. And so to bed, where — in keeping with the family precept which the Consul reads a few
pages later in the family book: 'be of good heart at your
business by day, but do only such business that we may sleep
quietly of nights' (2,1) — they, presumably, sleep quietly.

To work for the good of the family and to accumulate
money are normally synonymous activities, and the Consul
spends many happy years in their pursuit. When next,
however, he is torn between the conflicting claims of family,
money and Christian principle, he is head of the family and

obliged to play that role which his father played in the previous scene. On that occasion his father had made no secret of his opinions: now, however, in trying to bring Tony round to the point of insisting on separating from Grünlich, the Consul shows that he can play only with his cards hidden. The fact that Tony at first misreads his signals and assumes she is meant to play the role of devoted wife makes for the comedy of the scene. The Consul, as a member of the generation which has learnt to pay enthusiastic respect to human feelings (4,8) – we recall his father's sneers at this mixture of emotionalism and hard-nosed business sense (1,10) – is 'ratlos' (at a loss) when he confronts Tony's tears, exactly as he had been in the earlier scene when confronted by the appeal in Gotthold's accusing letter. Even Grünlich's sham tears give the Consul a moment of self-doubt and panicky emotionalism. His conscience is not easy, for he knows that, without his pressure, Tony's marriage would never have taken place. More profoundly, he has been hurt at the revelation of the underlying ruthlessness and brutality of the business world, the sudden coldness with which his 'friends' greet a man brushed by the wings of financial loss. He knows deep in his soul that civilisation built on business is a perilous undertaking, and that everyone is alone in the struggle for existence and survival. For all his enthusiasm for feelings, the Consul has reason to fear and distrust them: he suffers from being made vulnerable by them. Such experiences have dented his confidence, and he must work hard, both on himself and on Tony, for his success. Although his subtlety brings Tony safely home at no further expense to the firm – a result which 'every man', we are told, would take for granted (4,7) – it is precisely that emotional skill and that sensitivity of mind which have made him aware of the threatening forces at work in life, and thus made his own struggle harder. His weapons of survival are shown to contain the seeds of his own destruction.

It is characteristic that Thomas's first conflict with the family over money and obligation is a lost cause before it ever begins. His sister Clara has died, and the Konsulin has already given Clara's share of the family fortune to her husband Tibertius. Thomas can do no more than recriminate. We do not expect him to win the argument, but we look to understand with what weapons and with how much confidence he fights. The scene reveals the same truth the Consul learned: how little it profits a man materially to be emotionally and intellectually sensitive. Thomas's reputation as 'the least bourgeois and restricted mind' in the business community (6,7), his skill and acumen, his wide vision and sensitivity to the outside world have produced successes, but such success is purchased at a high price in terms of inner doubts, loss of confidence in the values which he is supposed to defend in the family. Thomas unmasks the nature of family relations: he sees the psychological mechanisms which lie behind family agreement (how Tiberius works on Christian to gain his support), and he must see through relationships and attitudes which, for the sake of family unity, were best accepted at face value. Worst of all, Thomas is obliged to concede that the argument has little to do with real interests (money), but is important to him for personal reasons, as part of a private campaign. What he had confessed earlier to Tony (7,6) is made manifest here: his fear of having lost his grip on events, his recognition that they are taking on a will of their own rather than conforming to his will. Previously things would never have 'dared' to defy his will, and the bitter row with his mother is not merely a rearguard action by means of which he cannot hope to regain the money, it is also in terms of the real forum of the action − Thomas's inner life − a show of token resistance only. Thomas's argument is conducted in the shadow of his father's actions, but the parallels can give him no confidence that he will win through. He did not hear his father comment to Johann that a house divided against itself will fall (1,10), but he echoes the sentiment exactly. While the Consul could with confidence (and advantage) commend Grünlich to pray (in consolation for the money he has refused him) (4,9), Thomas can pick up the gesture only at second hand, and it holds neither profit nor consolation for him. He ends the scene with the words: 'Were Father still alive, if he were with us here, he would put his hands together in prayer and commend us all to the mercy of God' (7,7).

Thomas's second conflict involves still more obviously a dilemma within himself rather than a conflict with members of the family. The date is 1868. Tony has visited a former schoolfriend, whose husband requested Thomas to buy the crops on his estate at Pöppenrade before the harvest, since he needs ready cash to meet his pressing gambling debts. Thomas immediately rejects the offer Tony supports as being inconsistent with the family's business standards and amounting, he feels, to exploitation of another's misfortune. Tony is disappointed, but Thomas flatters her sense of family pride with an anecdote to show his social equality with the landed gentry. The matter seems closed.

No sooner has Tony left Thomas than a major change takes place. The confident and elegant expression which Thomas puts on when dealing with the world, and with which he has just rejected his sister's suggestion, is shown to be a mask, and it slips off as his one recurring thought returns to haunt him: that at forty-two he is a broken and exhausted man. The massive discrepancy between his appearance and the state of his soul is revealed. Thomas's effort to hide his true self behind a meticulous exterior has given rise to the popular view of his 'vanity' (7,5; 10,3) and will become such that Thomas will be compared to an actor on the stage (10,1). What makes the talk of his vanity so hard to bear is that the truth is not merely whispered behind Thomas's back by rivals and colleagues (it is also pointed out to the reader by an omniscient narrator over his head): Thomas's own intelligence and self-awareness have made this truth quite manifest to him. We presume that Thomas realises what the narrator allows Thomas's valet to tell us: that he has become penny-pinching and mean, laughably inadequate to the representative role he imposes upon himself. Not only is Thomas cracking under the strain of keeping up appearances, holding in position that mask which has just slipped from his face; he has to watch himself engaged in that struggle with himself, and to accept that misfortune and failure have their roots not

in a business world which inflicts loss with one hand and gain
with the other, but are instead products of his own lack of
determination, of his 'notion that his good fortune and success were at an end, a notion which possessed only subjective
truth and had no basis in external fact' (8,4).

It is here that Tony has provoked him. His reply to her
offer had been unfitting, and she had seen that his resistance
to her proposition was the product of doubt, not of self-
assurance. Behind his response had lain what is increasingly
seen as the principal uncertainty of Thomas's life: 'Was
Thomas Buddenbrook a business man, a man of untram-
melled action − or a scruple-ridden dreamer?'

Like the question addressed to the gatekeeper in Kafka's
The Trial who guards one man's entrance to the Law, this
question is there only for Thomas. It has, we learn, haunted
him all his life. The link to the Consul is evident as we see how
self-doubt has risen up in Thomas at those moments when
life's brutality and inhumanity are revealed under the veneer
of civility. Thomas has felt this once before in the coldness
and mistrust which greeted him during the bankruptcy of a
Frankfurt bank in 1866. He encountered there in business life
something which he understands as a feature of life itself, for
business life is merely 'an image of the larger totality of life
itself' (8,4): the falling-away of all pleasantness and conven-
tionality as so much play-acting 'in the face of the single raw,
naked and domineering instinct of self-preservation'. This experience has hurt him even more than it had hurt his father.
How often he has had to 'correct' his personal emotions in
order to try to diminish the hurt: how he has wished to 'deal
out harshness to suffer harshness, and to *feel* it not as
harshness but as something natural'. How often, in short, has
his hurt longing that life be different taken the form of
pretending that he is different, doing violence to his real
nature, because he knows that life cannot be changed. This
is the conflict that has worn him out.

If Tony has offered him the first telling challenge, the
second is still more significant, for it came from his brother
Christian. Thomas recalls an occasion when he literally

dismissed Christian from the firm for having, in his Club, dropped a casual remark about all businessmen being crooks and deceivers (6,3). This remark had offended the ethical aspect of Thomas's business mind, precisely that part of him which had so sternly rejected Tony's suggestion to buy Maiboom's crops in the ear. Nevertheless, Christian has spoken that secret truth which Thomas has tried for so long to repress – namely that business, like life, is about ruthlessness and power – and the remark has challenged afresh Tom's efforts to 'correct' his feelings and to live up to life. The thought of Hagenström – his rival not only in business but in the image of vitality and energy which he projects to the world, a symbol in short of the ruthlessness behind life – taking this opportunity away from him is intolerable. Should Thomas stand aside scrupulously and watch his rival profit? So he takes up Tony's suggestion and embarks upon the deal he had begun by rejecting.

In the short term it seems successful: Thomas's gait regains its elegance and elasticity, his humour is restored, he even manages to make a fool of Hagenström at a public meeting. But the long-term consequences are catastrophic, for not only does the coup fail to make money – the crops are destroyed by a hailstorm – the still more speculative coup of 'correcting' his inner life draws heavily on the dwindling capital of Thomas's nervous energy and brings him still closer to collapse.

The final conflict, between Thomas and his brother, is more trivial than any of the others in terms of monetary values. Gotthold had argued for a hundred thousand, Thomas had gambled with half that sum, while Christian only wants crumbs from the table. Yet this conflict is the most bitter for it is the most openly conducted, since Christian, having remained outside much of the family ritual, sees it with appalling clarity and, worse still, sees Thomas with the damaging knowledge of the insider. Thomas has no chance to hide behind the protective clichés of family head, businessman, or believer, for his brother sees through them all no less clearly than he does himself. Thomas is pushed into a situation where his defence of the family must disclose itself, and in a revealing crescendo of reproaches he finds himself uncovering more and more profoundly his real motivation as head of the family and the real source of the determination with which he fights for family and firm. If, at earlier stages of the novel, the contrast between Thomas and Christian seemed to juxtapose success and failure, imaginative adaptation to society and the unproductive rejection of society, this scene makes it unmistakable that the contrast hides profound similarities, and from it Thomas by no means emerges victorious.

The scene contains many familiar elements, but they work together here with a new intensity. The heat of the argument has little in common with the kind of anger Thomas's grandfather felt when Gotthold married the shopkeeper, Demoiselle Stüwing. Although Christian's offence against family morality – his intention of marrying Aline Puvogel, the lady of questionable virtue with whom he was intimate in Hamburg – is much greater than Gotthold's had been, the family's behaviour is little affected by a sense of moral outrage. Tony's enjoyment of her new role as domestic supremo – the scene opens with her ostentatious prayer and closes with her lament about the fate of the family house – is too self-indulgent to enable her effectively to counter the substance of Christian's claims, while the argument soon makes clear (Thomas: ' "Perhaps I am more ill than you" ') that Thomas too is hardly fighting to win. The gradual clarification of these positions and the dramatic nature of the confrontation remind us of Thomas Mann's great ability to focus his intellectual and psychological themes in realistic human interaction, and we may also wonder whether the scene's dramatic power hints at the intensity of the personal experiences which Mann's novel had to digest.

'Christian!' stieß Frau Permaneder entsetzt hervor. 'Was sprichst du? . . . Mein Gott, worüber streitet ihr euch eigentlich? Ihr tut, als sei es eine Ehre, der Kränkere zu sein! Wenn es *darauf* ankäme, so hätten leider Gerda und ich auch noch ein Wörtchen mitzureden! . . . Und Mutter liegt nebenan . . .!'

'Und du begreifst nicht, Mensch', rief Thomas Buddenbrook leidenschaftlich, 'daß alle diese Widrigkeiten Folgen und Ausgeburten deiner Laster sind, deines Nichtstuns, deiner Selbstbeobachtung?! Arbeite! Höre auf, deine Zustände zu hegen und zu pflegen und darüber zu reden! . . . Wenn du verrückt wirst – und ich sage dir ausdrücklich, daß das nicht unmöglich ist –, ich werde nicht imstande sein, eine Träne darüber zu vergießen, denn es wird deine Schuld sein, deine allein . . .'

'Nein, du wirst auch keine Träne vergießen, wenn ich sterbe.'

'Du stirbst ja nicht', sagte der Senator verächtlich.

'Ich sterbe nicht? Gut, ich sterbe also nicht! Wir werden ja sehen, wer von uns beiden früher stirbt! . . . Arbeite! Wenn ich aber nicht kann? Wenn ich es nun aber auf die Dauer nicht kann, Herr Gott im Himmel?! Ich kann nicht lange Zeit dasselbe tun, ich werde elend davon! Wenn du es gekonnt hast und kannst, so freue dich doch, aber sitze nicht zu Gericht, denn ein Verdienst ist nicht dabei . . . Gott gibt dem einen Kraft und dem anderen nicht . . . Aber so bist du, Thomas', fuhr er fort, indem er sich mit immer verzerrterem Gesicht über den Tisch beugte und immer heftiger auf die Platte pochte . . . 'Du bist selbstgerecht . . . ach, warte nur, das ist es nicht, was ich sagen wollte und was ich gegen dich vorzubringen habe . . . Aber ich weiß nicht, wo ich anfangen soll, und das, was ich werde sagen können, ist nur der tausendste . . . ach, es ist nur der millionste Teil von dem, was ich gegen dich auf dem Herzen habe! Du hast dir einen Platz im Leben erobert, eine geehrte Stellung, und da stehst du nun und weisest kalt und mit Bewußtsein alles zurück, was dich einen Augenblick beirren und dein Gleichgewicht stören könnte, denn das Gleichgewicht, das ist dir das Wichtigste. Aber es ist nicht das Wichtigste, Thomas, es ist vor Gott nicht die Hauptsache! Du bist ein Egoist, ja, das bist du! Ich liebe dich noch, wenn du schiltst und auftrittst und einen niederdonnerst. Aber am schlimmsten ist dein Schweigen, am schlimmsten ist es, wenn du auf etwas, was man gesagt hat, plötzlich verstummst und dich zurückziehst und jede Verantwortung ablehnst, vornehm und intakt, und den anderen hilflos seiner Beschämung überläßt . . . Du bist so ohne Mitleid und Liebe und Demut . . . Ach!' rief er plötzlich, indem er beide Hände hinter seinen Kopf bewegte und sie dann weit vorwärts stieß, als wehrte er die ganze Welt von sich ab . . . 'Wie satt ich das alles habe, dies Taktgefühl und Feingefühl und Gleichgewicht, diese Haltung und Würde . . . wie sterbenssatt . . .' Und dieser letzte Ruf war in einem solchem Grade echt, er kam so sehr von Herzen und brach mit einem solchen Nachdruck von Widerwillen und Überdruß hervor, daß er tatsächlich etwas Niederschmetterndes hatte, ja, daß Thomas ein wenig Zusammensank und eine Weile wortlos und mit müder Miene vor sich niederblickte.

'Ich bin geworden, wie ich bin', sagte er endlich, und seine Stimme klang bewegt, 'weil ich nicht werden wollte wie du. Wenn ich dich innerlich gemieden habe, so geschah es, weil ich mich vor dir hüten muß, weil dein Sein und Wesen eine Gefahr für mich ist . . . ich spreche die Wahrheit.'   (9,2)

'Christian!' Frau Permaneder's [Tony's] voice was choked with horror, 'what are you saying? Oh God, what are you two arguing about anyway? You are behaving as if it is an honour to be more ill than the other. Anyway, if *that* were the point, then unfortunately Gerda and I would have a word or two of our own to say on that score? . . . And Mother is lying in the next room!'

'Don't you understand', shouted Thomas Buddenbrook passionately, 'that all these repulsive things are the result and product of your vices and your idleness and your obsession with yourself? Get down to some work! Stop cultivating your inner states and stop talking about them . . . If you go mad − and I tell you straight, that's not impossible − I shall not be able to shed a single tear over it, for it will be your fault and only your fault! . . .'

'No, you won't shed a tear when I die.'

'You won't die', said the Senator contemptuously.

'Won't I? All right, so I'm not going to die. We will see which of us dies first! . . . Get down to work? But suppose I can't, suppose I can't stick at my work for long? Good Lord, I just can't spend a long time doing the same thing: it makes me miserable. If you have been able to do that, and still can, then enjoy it, but don't sit in judgement, for there is no virtue in it . . . God gives strength to one man, and not to the next . . . But that's what you are like, Thomas,' he continued, leaning across the table and screwing up his face more and more, banging increasingly hard on the table-top . . . 'you're self-righteous . . . ah, just wait, that's not all I wanted to say, not the only accusation I have to make . . . But I don't know where to start, and what I shall manage to say is only a thousandth − no, only a millionth of what I have got against you in my heart. You have got yourself a place in life, a respected position, and there you sit, and coldbloodedly and deliberately you turn your back on anything that could for one moment put you off, disturb your balance − for your balance is the most important thing to you. But, Thomas, it is not the most important thing, God knows, it is not the main thing. You are an egoist, that's what you are. I still love you, even when you tell me off, give yourself airs and shout me down. But the worst thing of all is your silence, the worst thing is when you suddenly go quiet when someone has said something: you draw back, deny all responsibility, you act high and mighty and untouchable, and you leave the fellow to his embarrassment. You are so pitiless, so without love and humility . . . Ah!', he cried out suddenly, waving his hands behind his head and then thrusting them out in front of him as if he were trying to ward off the whole world . . . 'how sick I am of it all, all this tact and delicacy, this balance and correctness and respectability . . . sick to death of it all . . .' This last outburst was so genuine, it came so much from the heart, it came across in such a way as to make unmistakable Christian's tired and sated repulsion, that it did in fact have a crushing effect. So much so that Thomas subsided somewhat and sat for a while without speaking, staring down in front of him with a weary expression.

'I have become what I am', he said finally, in a voice that betrayed his emotion, 'because I did not want to become what you are. If I have shunned you inwardly, then it has been because I need to be on my guard against you, because your life and your character are a danger to me . . . I'm telling you the truth . . .'

Tony's initial intervention in this argument is disturbing enough. Her horror at this quarrel, her attempt to preserve some genuine family feeling, is immediately undone by her stupidity, as she joins in the competition in illness. It is not merely a silly competition, but she herself has never had a day's illness in her life. Yet she is not entirely wrong to identify Gerda with illness and decadence, even though she fails to see Tom's participation in this process. In her remarks insight and blindness are once again in balance. Her last phrase ('"And Mother is lying in the next room"') becomes a 'Leit-motiv' running through the scene to remind us of the demise of the family tradition − matched by the other recurring image in this scene, the 'mocking' look with which Gerda views the scene, coldly remote from an argument which perhaps she alone, with her special relationship to both parties, could have resolved.

Thomas picks up an old theme, the criticism of Christian's 'repulsive preoccupation with himself' which he has made before (6,2). In an earlier confrontation Thomas had accused Christian of excessive concern with self and with the 'nauseating *finesses*' of his inner life. This was the occasion when he had called Christian 'an unhealthy growth on the body of the family' (6,3). The present argument, however, will make clear that work and activity are not simply

Thomas's preferred values and life-style: they represent an escape from those very vices of Christian which Thomas knows all too well. Interesting too is the exchange of predictions and the tone in which it is conducted. Thomas is right about the insanity which awaits Christian, but no less revealing is the near pride with which he defends a genuine experience – death – as though it represented a value to which the *poseur*, Christian, has no right. He does more in this remark than express his view that Christian is not really ill: he implies that he is not fit for death.

When Christian speaks, he shows that he has not merely become acquisitive: he has no longer any reason to be silent about the insights he has gained into his brother. The scene, like the figure itself and his language ('a thousandth . . . a millionth') is exaggerated: Christian leans further and further over the table, a comic and even grotesque element, building on the absurdity of Tony's remarks, emphasised by Mann's characteristic use of the repeated dots after his sparse scene-setting. The scene is drawn in this way because Mann wants the reader to understand the psychological combat, not to be distracted by unnecessary external details: for the argument's content is deadly serious, summarising a conflict which has run throughout the novel.

What is striking in Christian's remarks is how well he reads his brother's character. He clearly recalls their earlier confrontation. The disgust with which Christian ends his speech is an extended version of that 'Pfui' (Shame on you) with which he broke off the previous dispute (6,3). At the same time, however, Christian knows things which we as readers have learned from conversations in which Christian did not participate. So, for instance, Thomas's assertion that for him balance was 'the main thing' had been made in a conversation with Tony which Christian had not heard (5,2). Tony had not really understood the point: she had thought that Thomas was attacking the Hagenströms. Christian, though absent, has understood. It is an example of Mann's use of dialogue to broaden and deepen the thematic development of the novel – a technique which Fontane used in his novels to great effect. Christian is also very close to the mark when he challenges Thomas to say that he enjoys his capacity for work, to take positive pleasure in what God has provided rather than to sit in judgement over those who cannot enjoy work. We, from our privileged position as readers, have by this stage abundantly observed Thomas's increasing difficulties in enjoying work: again Christian cannot know that his remark pains Thomas, but it highlights the actual state of mind of his brother with uncanny accuracy.

Christian's last remark and his last pose are the most evocative of all. The gesture again borders on the comic and grotesque (how hard to preserve in an English translation Mann's combination of natural language with psychological symbolism). Christian is indeed trying to keep at bay 'die Welt', the world itself with its duties, routine and roles to play, and it is this 'world' which he sees embodied in his brother. In the same way Thomas and his father saw in their world of business 'an image of the larger totality of life itself' (8,4); and Hanno will see school with 'revulsion, resistance and fear' (11,2) as a microcosm of the world. Christian's gesture eloquently summarises this whole attitude. At the same time we wonder whether he, who has successfully held reality at bay for so long, really can be so 'sick to death' of the world, and whether that weariness to death does not better describe the condition of his brother. Here, once more, a dialogue raises a possibility, varies a theme, which the reader, forced by the narrator to reflect, comes to associate with another character; thus the reader's understanding of the scene is enlarged beyond the narrower viewpoints of the characters themselves.

Christian has said some true things, but he has also exaggerated and once again over-dramatised himself. His feelings are both grotesque and genuine. In just the same way, the hypocrite Grünlich, forced for different reasons (as a man trying to avoid bankruptcy) to live off the spurious and the unreal, appears both grotesque and paradoxically genuine when he rather desperately tries to force Tony to accept him in marriage, and again just before her final departure, when he tries to save that marriage. Even he, to Tony's 'surprise' (4,9), manages to touch real emotion. So Christian's remarks, for all their theatricality, have something genuine and 'crushing' about them.

Thomas, in his reply, shows why he was struck dumb, why his look is 'weary' as he hears of Christian's tiredness with life. He must admit that he has become what he is in order not to become like Christian — and, fundamentally, for no other reason. Christian's nature and way of life represent a danger to Thomas, because they show him not only what he might become, but also what he is: a man living by tokens, artificially. The chief of those artificial goals — Christian had once called them 'counter-ideas' (6, 3) — had been not to resemble Christian, and the futility of Tom's striving is made clear in the course of the argument. This scene demonstrates the extent to which the family's firmness of purpose has been undermined, weakened by self-awareness, by an intellectual understanding imperfectly attuned both to profit-making and to the attainment of real goals, and by emotional and moral sensitivity. These are the elements that move the novel's focus so far from purely economic issues and give it such a strong psychological emphasis.

Our understanding of the nature of this development is confirmed by the figure of Hanno, who marks the family's final decline. The reader is struck by the fact that no purely biological argument is sufficient to account for Hanno's character and role: biological weakness follows on intellectual insights, but does not — as in the naturalist viewpoint — initiate them. We are not dealing with a degenerate weakling, inadequate to the challenges which life issues, but with an increasingly deliberate rejection of these challenges. If he fails to participate in life, Hanno does so consciously and in full knowledge of the consequences, and in so doing proves to be the true son of his father. He is marked by precocious intelligence (this, as Mann's letter to Grautoff suggested, was not necessarily part of the musical inheritance, see p. 29). From his earliest days Hanno clearly understands the nature of the world and the family into which he is born. The effect of his understanding, however, is to alienate him from the role which family convention allots to him as male successor. He asks himself the question that had plagued his father but, in contrast to Tom, Hanno calmly assents to the answer he reaches: namely, that he is not suited to be a 'man of action', and that his emotional sensitivity disqualifies him for the business world and for the life of which it is a symbol. He feels no need to correct his feeling and fit himself for the world. He rejects the world, and opts for death as the way out.

It is here that the musical theme of the novel is integrated into the family's history of increasing intellectual refinement and sensitivity. Indeed, music's role is to represent the triumph of the family's detachment from the service of practical, business-orientated goals. It is no coincidence that the culmination of the family's decline is reached in its most musical member, Hanno. With hindsight we recall the Consul's reluctance to go to the billiard-room with the gentlemen after dinner and to forgo the chance of listening to music in the other room and 'indulging in his dreams and feelings' (1,8). He obviously prefers music and the dreaming which accompanies it to the diet of dubious jokes and coarse sociability with the 'men of action'. His tastes are passed on to his son in the form of his susceptibility to literature and philosophy. It may seem that music misses out Thomas's generation (certainly he hates the sense of being excluded from the music world in which Gerda moves) but, as Gerda points out in a suggestive phrase, even the unmusical Buddenbrooks have musical hands: they are born for music, therefore, without realising it. Music belongs in the family tradition, and with time it emerges fully.

It is important to distinguish this musical element in the family from mere facility at playing a musical instrument. In the earlier generations (Johann's flute playing, accompanied by his daughter-in-law) music had fulfilled a function within the family: it had been socially useful. In much the same way Jean Jacques Hoffstede, court-poet to the patrician circles of Lübeck, had fulfilled a direct social function with his occasional verses. Only with the passing of the generations and the changes this entails do such accomplishments become problematic, as is made clear in the scene in which Hoffstede's successor, the broker Gosch, is so influenced by his reading about revolution (like Flaubert's Frédéric Moreau he finds the masses 'superb') that he cannot *act* at all when confronted by the reality of revolution (4,7). Hanno's music – in its isolation from society, its attainment of intensity and expression beyond the common reach – participates in the gradual separation of the arts from society; Mann approaches music, like everything else, in the spirit of historical analysis.

The improvisation which is almost the last act of Hanno's life shows the culmination of all these tendencies. It is carefully prepared for by the account of Hanno's school-day (11,2). For Hanno school represents life itself, the world as will in microcosm, and he looks upon his world 'full of revulsion and wounded beyond cure', just as his father had done (8,4). From this world of misery music offers escape and compensation. The improvisation, this simple motif which (in deliberate contrast to a world which is all too real) is almost nothing, has an intensity which is obviously sexual, and moves towards the only kind of emotional fulfilment and climax Hanno knows. It marks the end of the link between the Buddenbrooks' emotions and their business success. There has been talk between Hanno and Kai, his only school friend, of the problems of adolescence, and the improvisation reveals clearly the introverted sexuality and autoeroticism which are its principal driving-force. Music is both the triumph and sensitivity in the Buddenbrooks and the culmination of their psychological decay.

The particular music which Gerda and Hanno bring into the Buddenbrooks' world is, of course, the music of Wagner and, as its quintessential example, *Tristan and Isolde*. In his own life, Thomas Mann had always seen Wagner's work as representing art's concern with the exotic, the sensual and faraway. The silvery sheen of *Lohengrin*, which Hanno found so enchanting; the Dutchman ever wandering, pulling Senta away from the everyday world; the radical break between life and the wondrously evoked world of love, and of night and death in *Tristan and Isolde* — these were the constitutive experience of Mann's youthful relationship to art. Nevertheless, the arrival of Wagner in the Buddenbrook circle is shown to be more than a domestic or purely personal event. Not only the family is disconcerted by the problematic nature of this new art, so different from the manageable emotions of after-dinner music; the musical establishment itself shares the sense of outrage. When Gerda puts Wagner's music in front of Edmund Pfühl, organist of the Marienkirche and guardian of a more functional music, three centuries of tradition rise in rebellion. Pfühl's rejection of *Tristan* echoes the comments of Wagner's notorious critic, Hanslick, who had written of the dangers of the 'unhealthy stimulation' of Wagner's music, and the reader initially refers these comments simply to the role Gerda's decadent music plays in the family. But the scene develops in such a way as to suggest that this decadence has a place within a wider tradition. In an amusing seduction scene, Pfühl's complaints at the music gradually give way to admiration and to a recognition that in fact Wagner belongs in the tradition Pfühl represents, just as, in a profound sense, Hanno's music belongs in the Buddenbrook family. The decadence which undermines the order comes from within.

It is part of the undercurrent of personal tragedy in the novel that Hanno's qualities do not consistently bring him close to his father, who shares so many of them. Hanno finds in music a particular refuge from his problems: it is one from which Thomas is completely excluded. What divides them has a deeper cause than music, however, and, just as it was Christian's affinities with Thomas which led to their alienation, so it is with Hanno. Thomas is incapable of teaching Hanno a faith in the world which he does not possess himself, and incapable of forming a new life round the knowledge that they share. As he takes Hanno on the social round, hoping to introduce him to the world in which he is to play a major part, the effect is the opposite, for Hanno — like his father in other situations — sees more than is good for him. He recognises the whole performance which Thomas puts on for the play-

acting it is; he sees the cost but can detect no purpose behind
it. Should this charade be the goal of man's life, he wonders;
does anything lie behind it, or is it just 'an end in itself'
(10,2)? What his grandfather saw only in clairvoyant
moments of crisis is a daily experience for Hanno: the
recognition that the daily business of life is a facade, behind
it emptiness and suffering. How is it possible, he asks, 'to
recognise a situation, to see through it, and then despite
everything to exploit that situation with no sense of shame'?.
If that is what is meant by 'Lebenstüchtigkeit' (being fit for
life) (10,2), if it is that which Thomas wants to achieve by
'correcting' Hanno's feelings (he calls it 'hardening him up'),
then Hanno wants none of it and at the end of his life
deliberately assents to that half-conscious action when, as a
child, he had drawn a final line through the family book (8,7).
'I can't will anything', he remarks to Kai; there is no happiness for him in a world he is condemned 'to see through
with such nauseating clarity', and no belief that it might be
changed (11,2). Thomas might have said the same, but only
in that searing moment of truth when he and Hanno meet on
the common ground of suffering − Thomas being in agonies
of doubt and existential pain as he waits outside the silent
music room − only then, for a fleeting instant, do their
similarities bring them together. But this persona, the real
Thomas, is the one doomed to lose out in the struggle for life,
and all he can bequeath to his son are the inner dynamics of
his own decline.

Chapter 6

Thomas Buddenbrook

We saw how, in the evolution of the novel, the introspective memories of the sensitive late-comer Hanno were integrated into a wider span of civic and family history. In the course of this shift, one generation came to be central to the compressed timescale of the novel — that of Thomas, Christian and Tony. Within this generation Mann's major interest clearly lies with Thomas.

What makes Thomas interesting is that he responds to the problems he shares with Christian by endeavouring to maintain in his life that 'self-control [Haltung] and balance' (5,2) which Christian so completely lacks. At the same time, Thomas's choice of Gerda as partner — and this, as we suggested, is the point at which his fortune deserts him and the family's decline is sealed — has its origins in a desire to be different, to be more distinguished than his generation in Lübeck, not to marry 'some silly teenager from the Möllendorpf — Langhals — Kistenmaker — Hagenström set' (5,7): in short, what moves him is that self-important family pride ('the feeling of personal importance') that is at the heart of Tony's beliefs and actions too. It is the memory of this feeling that haunts Thomas at the end of his life: 'Repeatedly, when the hours of melancholy came upon him, Thomas Buddenbrook would ask himself what he in fact still was that might justify his having even a slightly higher opinion of himself than of any one of his more simply constituted, stolid fellow citizens with their petty bourgeois limitations' (10,1). If, as it surely does, the novel suggests an answer to this question, it is to be found in the consequentiality with which Thomas attempts to confront the legacy his family has bequeathed to him and in the complex balance of the solutions he attempts.

More specifically, the reason why Thomas is interesting is that, in marked contrast to Christian and Tony, he passes through a development. Christian's die is cast from the first pages of the novel, as 'fool' (1,2) and actor, sickly and self-indulgent. It takes time for him to pass from prosperity to the asylum in which he ends his days, but only time. Tony too, in her desire to please, her pert charm and her sense of what is proper, does not change during the novel − it is this lack of change that makes her ageing so painful and funny. Once her decision to marry Grünlich has been taken, her life is like that toboggan journey down the Jerusalem Hill she thinks of on the first page of the novel: it has its own momentum and direction. Thomas not only develops in himself: our relationship to him and knowledge of him develop constantly.

At the beginning of his career as head of the firm, Thomas seemed ambitious and eager, perfectly suited to his position. As he sat awaiting details of his father's will, 'the longing for action, victory and power, the desire to force good-fortune to her knees burned in his eyes briefly and violently' (5,1). His confidence that he could master the situation was clearly justified, and he soon learned to exploit his personal charm and elegance in 'the daily struggle for success' (5,3). When Gotthold had died, Thomas felt confident enough to draw the lessons of his uncle's unsuccessful life and to view in a distanced and yet positive way the process of 'die Dehors wahren' (keeping up appearances) − that cluster of conventions which even the 'suitors' observe but which Gotthold had neglected − to recognise the limitations set on one's life, but by 'imagination and idealism' to transcend them. In the drive for pre-eminence within the small world of Lübeck, to be 'a Caesar in a modest trading-town on the Baltic', Thomas found both purpose and poetry (5,4). He has the intellectual flexibility to achieve this, and to philosophise on the topic to his less charismatic colleagues. To be the intellectually most gifted member of his business circle was useful not simply in order to impress Stephan Kistenmaker, and to shine in society: it opened Thomas's eyes to possibilities in business, to ways of overcoming the provincial outlook of Lübeck's tradition-ridden business community. From the start he has prided himself on the ability 'simultaneously to belittle, and to take seriously, his ambition of achieving greatness and power in his restricted sphere' (6,7), but this intellectuality, amounting almost to a double-life, bears the seed of its own destruction. With growing scepticism he watches himself perform his familiar ritual of self-motivation through external, token goals. The new house, the election to Senator, the clinging to money and prestige — these objectives are increasingly understood to be the shell in which he hopes his wandering sense of purpose may find refuge. 'Senator' and 'House' are externals, they are not the substance, but the shapes into which substance might flow — this in a conversation with Tony (7,6) — or, to quote Christian, they are the 'counter-ideas' with which Thomas hopes to defeat that unnamed idea to which he confesses only at the end: that he too is a decadent. Perhaps he enjoys all his ambitions more in the expectation than in the experience, 'the pleasure of anticipation is, as ever, the best thing' (7,6) knowing that 'good fortune and success are inside us' (7,6) rather than external agencies which one may 'force to their knees'; but this is to prefer, like Christian, the imagined to the real, the inner conceit to the external struggle. Worse still, Thomas is forced to be aware of these mechanisms, and — as in the Pöppenrade episode — to curse that fate which has chosen him to bear these insights. 'Was *he* called to express this thought, to consider it, even to come across it?' (8,4). He begins by wanting not to know those things in himself which might interfere with business acumen: he ends by suffering from those very skills which have given him business success: the ability to work the system that comes from the intellectual power to 'see through it' — a phrase which, we recall, is Hanno's (11,2).

Clearly these changes in Thomas are wrought at the cost of much suffering. While Christian tells everyone about his affliction, it takes a much keener eye to see Thomas's suffering. Apart from Hanno, only the narrator sees Thomas's sensitiveness clearly, and only occasionally does he show its symptoms. He hints in an early scene that Thomas was 'accustomed through illness to observe the manifestations of his nerves' (4,11) — Thomas also admits to Tony that he has himself known 'the anxious, vain and inquisitive preoccupation' with himself (5,2), but claims to have overcome such concern for self. We see Thomas's sensitivity in his severity with others, but most of all in the determined efforts Thomas makes to correct his own feelings, 'sich korrigieren' (6,chs.1,4), to bring himself so into line with life that he will no longer suffer from its hardness (8,4). It is this struggle, this 'an sich arbeiten' (working on himself) (7,5) which wears him out; it is pain which he attempts to conceal behind the mask of his 'vanity'. Thomas consciously refuses to withdraw into his suffering, like Christian, and is too intelligent to go forward unreflecting into pointless battle, like Tony. For the one he is too ethically-minded, for the other too intelligent. In his situation only suffering can possess both ethical and (as he finally learns) intellectual justification, and it increasingly becomes his chosen realm.

Thomas does not merely suffer from his nerves; his suffering comes from the fact that he fails to be himself and lives a lie, behind an artificial mask. He has obviously repressed all ambition to be himself, and, although, on one level, he knows this, his philosophy of life has always been to say that there were 'things happening inside you — processes which a sensible man does not bother himself with at all, which he simply wants to know nothing about' (5,2). We may sympathise with this attitude as a sensible, defensive reaction to Christian's 'nauseating preoccupation with self', but only up to a point, for it is dangerously ambiguous. It can mean a disciplined dedication to the practical and real, a commitment to producing the outward forms of behaviour and commercial activity despite inner uncertainties. But it evidently also means for Thomas a wilful ignorance about himself, a loss of his 'true self', a price too high to pay for any business success. Vogt finds confirmation in a remark of Schopenhauer's to the effect that nothing can be 'more absurd than to base one's life on the ambition to be something other than one is' (Vogt, 85).

This is certainly the dark side of Thomas's 'self-control and balance'.

Thomas's full secret is out by the beginning of Part Ten. The opening chapter takes the reader for the first time into that actor's dressing-room in which all Thomas's appearances, inside and outside the family, are planned and costumed, and exposes the little strategies and ruses of Thomas's public persona. His grandfather's house, in which the novel opened, demonstrated the integration of individual, society and business, containing under one roof the firm's store-rooms, large rooms for representative family and social functions, and others for recreation. Thomas's house is different, but not just in style. This luxurious house of the new generation, a lonely house without animation and movement which Thomas built with a Turkish proverb in mind — 'When the house is ready, death comes' (7,6) — has at its core only an actor's dressing-room, and has become, like the other trappings of Thomas's life, an outer shell, a 'Dehors' without substance, a piece of scenery.

Thomas not only enjoys a particular prominence in the novel's plot: he stands in a particular relationship to the narrator. While the narrator remains some way outside the character of Christian, only very rarely venturing into his mind; and while the narrator's only sign of his sympathy for Tony is, as we saw, not to enquire too closely into her motives and values, the narrator's response to Thomas is much closer than to either of these. So much of Thomas's part of the novel takes place within his — Thomas's — mind, in his unspoken aspirations, reflections and fears, that there comes to be an affinity between the very diction and cast of mind of narrator and character. It is no surprise to have Thomas Mann refer subsequently to Thomas Buddenbrook as being related to him in three ways: as a portrait of his own father, as a self-portrait, and as a literary creation (XII,71). It is not that the text lacks distance in its portrayal of Thomas: there is much clinically precise analysis of his vanity, his 'mask', his actor's life, much telling observation of his failures towards Hanno, and of his lapses in sensitivity where he should be

at his most sensitive. Rather, the novel repeatedly seems to
develop along the lines Thomas creates for himself. Thus it
remains, in regard to Gerda's passion for music, or Tony's
petty social snobbery, or Christian's precise feelings – let
alone his actual doings outside the family circle – at a
distance which exactly corresponds to Thomas's own tastes
and judgements. The novel's plot follows Thomas's search
for ultimate answers without suggesting alternative routes he
should follow (although it does remain at a critical distance),
and gives this search a unique prominence. The novel is not
Thomas's (any more than it remained the story of the sensitive late-comer Hanno), but by its focus and questioning it
belongs more nearly to Thomas than to anyone else.

The narrator's readiness to take the reader down the same
paths as Thomas is nowhere greater than in the celebrated
fifth chapter of Part Ten. In this chapter Thomas Buddenbrook reads what is obviously chapter 41 of the second
volume of Schopenhauer's main work, *The World as Will
and Imagination* (first published in 1844). The title of this
chapter is that given in the text: 'On Death and its relation to
the indestructibility of our true nature'. Schopenhauer's argument in this chapter is that the only lasting human endeavour
is rewarded in the species rather than in the individual, that
the individual's fear of death is unnecessary, for immortality
can be attained only to the extent that one is freed from individual will and can recognise it as part of the eternal will to
life represented by the 'World' and, more specifically, by the
human race. Thomas reads the philosopher as promising
escape from the intolerable double effort of trying to live up
to his public persona *and* working for the continuation of
himself and of the firm (the vehicle of his effort) in the person
of his son Hanno. His notion of self is revealed to him in its
narrowness: as a prison-house within which he suffers, and
his tears are shed in the joy of seeing the bars vanish by no
other effort than a change of perspective. He has read: 'Dying
is the moment of liberation from the one-sidedness of an
individuality which does not constitute the innermost core of
our being, but is rather to be thought of as an aberration'.

The chapter is taken from a large and systematic work, which it neither necessarily typifies nor summarises. Nevertheless, with book open on Thomas's lap, so to speak, we may briefly touch on the striking affinity between Schopenhauer's system and the themes of *Buddenbrooks* as reflected in Thomas's experiences.

The central argument of Schopenhauer's work is given in his title: that the world can be experienced in two ways, as will and as imagination. The world as will is that ceaseless struggle for existence in which people spend their energies, asserting themselves as individuals, striving and competing for illusory happiness and success. It is this world as will of which Thomas (and his father before him) sees in business life the partial reflection. However much the will may be identified with individual goals (the family firm, success and prestige in society), it not only transcends all individual aims, being the ultimate reality behind the world of appearances, but it is indifferent to goal or purpose, a 'blind, unstoppable impulse'. On the other side there is the world as imagination − not intellect, for the intellect is an instrument of the will and is subservient to it, but an imaginative capacity ('Vorstellung'), in its higher forms aesthetic and philosophical contemplation, the ability of the mind to abstract itself from willing and to see things beyond the veil of illusion for what they really are. This can be achieved only by renouncing world as will, renouncing it so radically that in fact individuation itself, the act of saying 'I', is surrendered: 'to the extent that the individual recognises an idea', Schopenhauer writes, understanding 'idea' in a Platonic sense as the eternal face of unchanging truth, 'he is no longer an individual'. Schopenhauer has in mind the surrender of self by the ascetic and mystic, but also that of the artist who reaches a supra-personal vision of the world. To know the truth sets us free from the tyranny of the will, but the freedom from will involves a denial of the will to individual life.

To consider the appropriateness of Schopenhauer to the final days of Thomas Buddenbrook raises both text-internal and historical issues: why a philosophical episode of this intensity should be vouchsafed him at the end of his life, and why that experience should be of Schopenhauer's philosophy. Thomas's acquaintance with Schopenhauer is anything but accidental (indeed, Schopenhauer's popularity at the end of the nineteenth century makes it a typical experience), even beyond the obvious and immediate cause − that Thomas is suffering from the fear of death and the issue of personal immortality that Schopenhauer so directly raises is anything but academic to him. Schopenhauer met that painful insight which, throughout his life, Thomas could only repress: that the goal to which he was devoting his life and energy, his individual 'will', was ultimately pointless. He had felt this intuitively but had always suppressed the insight by a fresh frenzy of willing, driving himself by intellectual tricks into willing the next stage of his life, and fearing above all that withdrawal from willing which he sees in his brother and then, to his horror, in his son. We can see how, at the end of his life, Thomas would welcome Schopenhauer with tears of joy.

Another reason for Thomas's attraction to Schopenhauer is suffering: Thomas's perennial experience, for which Schopenhauer gives a theoretical foundation. In Schopenhauer's system, to live in the world as will means to suffer. For the individual, suffering is part of the very process of individuation, part of the self's creation of particular needs and the unceasing effort to fulfill them − an effort which is futile because the will knows neither rest nor fulfilment. It is irrelevant which motives (firm, family, social status) lie behind the striving which Schopenhauer shows by its very nature to lead to suffering; motive is merely the form which the will has temporarily adopted − 'what matters is that the will is exercised at all [daß überhaupt gewollt wird] and with what degree of intensity'. Suffering is a product of the experience in the limitations of time and space of that will which is behind everything, of the basic human condition, of individuation itself, and it does not come from the inadequacy or weakness of any particular individual. We can understand the satisfaction with which Thomas realises that his suffering has been brought into a system, and – so to speak – justified.

The relationship to suffering distinguishes Thomas from the value-system in which he has been brought up. We have observed his growing frustration with the traditional family approach to matters of metaphysics, his scorn for easy piety based on illusion and for accepted religious attitudes which have left him in a state of 'spiritual immaturity and unpreparedness' (10,5). Thomas's encounter with Schopenhauer is narrated in terms of a religious experience – down to the liturgical language in which these moments are presented ("And behold: [. . .]") – that his enthusiasm for the philosophy has to be seen as a substitute for the metaphysical gap which his upbringing has left him. It is also Thomas's determination to see suffering as a metaphysical problem that makes him despise his brother and gives him so much greater seriousness of mind than his sister.

One feature of the Schopenhauer chapter of *Buddenbrooks* is particularly striking, and – in view of Schopenhauer's praise for those who deny the will – surprising: that Thomas ends his reading of a chapter, whose message is that it is good to give up the individual will, by affirming not only life in general, but that 'I' behind it, the source of all individual willing and suffering. Thomas must have misread Schopenhauer if he imagines that it is an invitation to continue the dance of life. As we shall see, Thomas Mann was ready to explain how this shift of mood came about, in terms of his own biography, and the issue is much discussed in the secondary literature. But Mann's subsequent explanations leave out the central issue, on which his text is unambiguous; how such a misreading was possible for Thomas Buddenbrook. We recognise the key sentence in Thomas's response to Schopenhauer as: 'Have I ever hated life, this pure, cruel and strong life? Foolishness and misunderstanding! I have only ever hated myself because I could not bear it. But I love you, I love all of you, you happy ones!' (10,5). Here Thomas Buddenbrook reverts, even at this supreme moment of life, to the self-destructive routine we have seen before, and 'corrects his feelings' by the standards of 'Life'. Once more he represses his own sensitivity and tries to emulate − to 'love' − that which he is not, inverting his projected vision of the ideal. The episode of the Pöppenrade harvest was Thomas's last major attempt at this psychological gymnastic: 'Often enough since his youth he had had to correct his feelings in the face of "Life" . . . To deal out harshness, to suffer harshness, and not to *feel* it as harshness but as natural − would he never learn that?' To be cruel, because life is cruel; to delight the happy and to bring the unhappy to despair, that wish which has its origins in Thomas's memory of Gosch's false envy of him for his supposed happiness (9,4) surfaces for the final time. Thomas cannot be content to let life be one thing and himself another, or stand back from a vitality in which he does not participate, himself weaker, more suffering. So once more he tries to climb aboard 'Life' under a false flag.

Here we have the clue to why Thomas dies so shortly after this scene. Not only do we feel that once Thomas has faced up to the whole truth about the life he leads (even more radically than in the row with his brother) he has destroyed all basis for the illusions he needs to sustain the effort of living on. Thomas, like Hanno, becomes an illustration of Schopenhauer's idea that to know fully is to surrender individuation. But it is no less important to see this as an echo of the Pöppenrade episode, a final drawing on the capital of his 'correctability'.

We have so far read the scene without considering factors outside the text. Schopenhauer's ideas were widely influential at the turn of the century, when, among other things, they served as a philosophical underpinning for cultural pessimism. In fact, the last thirty years of the nineteenth century represented the high point of Schopenhauer's reception — more so than the generation in which he wrote. Nevertheless, although the general tenets of Schopenhauer's philosophy might have been familiar to Thomas Mann's reader, this episode in the novel was read much as we have tried to, that is with psychological insight but little philosophical expertise. We should, however, with the advantage of hindsight, be aware that, on the level of history of

ideas (with which Thomas Mann was perhaps a little too
enamoured), the section raises much critical debate.

Discussions have started from Mann's subsequent suggestion that the appropriateness of Schopenhauer to the novel
stems from his encounter with *The World as Will and Imagination* in the autumn of 1899, when, in an intoxication
similar to Thomas's, he gulped down this philosophy 'for
days on end'. Mann's account of this episode concludes with
the claim that he incorporated his reading experience into the
manuscript of *Buddenbrooks*, 'which had just reached the
point at which Thomas Buddenbrook had to be brought to his
death' (XII,72f). This 'instrumental' view of the role of
Schopenhauer in the text is taken up strongly by T. J. Reed
(82). Frizen goes much further, showing on the evidence of
the Notebooks that Mann knew Schopenhauer much more
fully than Mann himself had claimed (Frizen, 38ff,76ff,492ff:
Vogt gives an account of this argument on p.80f); while Erich
Heller in a rightly celebrated chapter on *Buddenbrooks* offers
an interpretation of the entire novel in terms of
Schopenhauer's system. Expressing the central formula of the
plot − the decline of the will in the face of increasing reflective consciousness, culminating in the total rejection of the
will in music, the art-form most removed from reality −
Heller suggests that the entire novel stands to Schopenhauer's
philosophy as the *Divina Commedia* does to Thomas
Aquinas' theology: that the philosophy is source and 'syntax'
of the plot, that the novel is a brilliant exegetic act on a
canonical text.

Such debates are continued in critics' account of that rever-
sal of Schopenhauer's direction of argument which takes
place at the end of Thomas's vision. We have already suggested the psychological background to such a shift: but
behind it is also a question as to Thomas Mann's sources. We
observed in Thomas's attitudes at the end of the vision an ap-
parently indestructible love for life, an unlimited enthusiasm
for the 'game', despite the fact that he has often seen through
it and has had that insight authoritatively confirmed by
Schopenhauer. It is this love that expresses itself in that boy

who will be born 'well endowed and comely [. . .] cruel and
cheerful, one of those people the sight of whom increases the
happiness of the fortunate and drives the unfortunate to
despair: That is my son. *That is me*' (10,5). This is not
Schopenhauer at all — although it is a half quotation from
him — the source of this affirmation of life is recognisably
Nietzsche, and Thomas has invoked a scaled down version
of the blond beast, the one who says 'I'. Once again Mann
encourages the biographers, commenting on the breaking in
of Nietzschean ideas into a Schopenhauerian text (IX,561).
Erich Heller is among those critics who follow this hint, referring to Mann's 'creative indecision between the extremes of
Schopenhauer and Nietzsche' (p.65). Other critics are less certain that, at the time of writing the novel, Mann differentiated as clearly between two complex philosophical systems
as his subsequent writings imply, and Frizen questions
whether Mann was not in fact attempting (over-ambitiously)
a conflation or synthesis of the two philosophies (p.94).

In considering these issues, the reader of the novel (as
distinct from the historian of ideas) will have in mind the relationship between the text and its various more or less
autobiographical sources. We have seen that the text works
over Mann's personal experiences, presenting them in a
distanced and analytical way, as if they too are 'documents'
which must be integrated into the overall structure of the
novel. The Nietzschean element in the text is no different: its
treatment confirms the text's insistence on pursuing, here too,
its critical method. In any case, Nietzsche's attraction for
Mann did not lie in any system, but in Nietzsche's skill in a
type of psychological acumen which Mann had always
cultivated (we recall his early description of himself as a
master of the 'psychological short story') and which he continued in *Buddenbrooks*. In that section of *Ecce Homo* when
'the psychologist speaks up', Nietzsche praised himself for his
'petit fait vrai' ('little truth'): the ability to infer from the
thought to its originator, from the idea back to its motivation, and it is this, the very essence of the novel's analytical
approach to character and experience, which marks the

presentation of Thomas Buddenbrook's philosopical encounters, and allows it to be integrated into the more mundane events of the novel.

Later in his literary career, in *Death in Venice*, Thomas Mann was to see in a figure such as Thomas Buddenbrook a hero of his own class, representative of the heroism Gustav von Aschenbach's works celebrate. It is remarkable how little of this heroism is expressed openly in the novel, despite Mann's claims for its representativeness. This is in part due to the distancing which the text undertakes, as Mann moved away from personal experience to the 'naturalist novel' which his text became. It is also related to ideological questions — an avoidance of the kind of uncritical hero-worship which was found in many novels of commercial life in the tradition of Gustav Freytag's *Soll und Haben* (1855), or the tendency towards heroicising in the manner of the pious family or municipal chronicle. No less important, however, is the narrator's readiness to accept Thomas's own assessment of himself: for instance, as Thomas passes the peak of his life and achievements, 'if, as he added to himself, it was at all possible in so mediocre and lowly a life to speak of a high-point' (10.1). The withdrawn modesty is Thomas's and it informs the whole novel. Christian and Tony could never have taken over the task of narrating the novel, lacking respectively the energy and the insight. Perhaps, as many critics have suggested, Kai (Hanno's school-friend) is its author. But the reason Thomas himself did not write it was because he invested in his own life, in the exterior he presented to the world, that organisational energy and reflective insight which the novel itself possesses. We should think of Thomas Mann as Thomas Buddenbrook freed from the constraints of societal representation and liberated for the work of art.

Chapter 7

Narrative technique

We turn in this section to consider the fabric of the novel's text and to examine more closely the way in which its themes and concerns are embedded in the narrative. We must not expect to find the stages of the story's evolution preserved like fossil layers in the final text. It is questionable whether such fossil layers could be established, even if the manuscript had survived, but they would in any case add little to our reading of a text whose nature − clearly stamped by that intellectualising which represented the third stage of the text's evolution − is to work over and analyse everything which it communicates. Both the perspective of the 'sensitive late-comer' and that of the 'municipal chronicle' are preserved, but both are orchestrated into a multiplicity of perspectives, which are played off against each other and relativised in their claims to truth. The only perennial feature of Mann's narrative stance is that it is always changing, and that no position is accepted as providing the exclusive perspective of the novel.

Point of view

A clear example of this shifting perspective can be found in the opening section of Part Seven, which deals with Hanno's christening, or rather − for that is the perspective with which the chapter opens − with what turns out to be Tony's christening. The first sentence sets the excitement of the event: 'Christening! . . . A christening in Broad Street!' What we are then shown is everything 'that Madame Permaneder had, in hopeful days, dreamt of beholding'. It is she who registers the scene, so much so that the description strays into sharing Tony's worry that 'hopefully' there is enough food on the laden tables, and her self-reassurance that 'there's no doubt about it' – the celebration has been worthily prepared. This perspective culminates in Tony's challenge to the outside world to share her sense of the importance of the occasion – 'An heir! A first-born son! Can anyone understand what that means?' Yet even through this insider view of events the reader cannot fail to notice another pair of eyes at work. Would Tony notice Ida Jungmann's snobbish gestures as she decks the table, head held aesthetically to one side and fingers most refinedly spread out? Would Tony describe the baby as 'a little something disappearing beneath lace and satin bows', or would her ear catch the vowel sounds and oddly rolled 'r' of a pastor anxious to please his wealthy parishioners? Above all, Tony could not understand the significance of the blue shadows under Hanno's eyes: it is the narrator who makes this detail suggestive. To combine narrative omniscience with the more limited viewpoint of Tony creates both the truth and the humour of the scene and makes it clear that Mann's narrative aim is the communication not of empathy, but of knowledge.

The same technique can be seen in the delightful chapter which introduces the events of 1848. It begins, as do many, with direct speech and at the dinner table, as the Consul enquires of his wife the reason for her apparent distress. The narrator quickly supplies minimal information on who is sitting at the table and then retires, allowing the Consul's thoughts to take over the narration, with his worries over the political situation in Schleswig-Holstein. The Consul then assimilates his wife's account of a mutiny in the kitchen. He does not simply listen, he modifies what his wife tells him, replacing overdramatic phrases (which the reader does not hear) with distanced, ironic phrases of his own. The butcher who incited the cook to mutiny enters the text as this 'perennially bloody' figure, a phrase which is neither the Konsulin's, for she is too upset to be ironic, nor the narrator's, but the Consul's. The cook's colourful prophecy of the imminent overthrow of the social order comes across directly, but the response ('Of course she was given notice at once') is not ascribed to any one character. The explicit assumption that the reader will agree with this course of action makes clear that the narrator is refraining from comment. The Consul shakes his head, and through his mind pass the events of a turbulent year of Lübeck politics, yet recalled in a linguistic register more elevated than a stream of consciousness or recorded thoughts: 'the new spirit of revolt had found a way insidiously to gain admission'. Since the narrator is not filling in the 'background', he feels no obligation to explain everything, indeed he can allow the Consul the luxury of a comment on those who had called for 'Universal suffrage on the basis of social status' − 'perhaps they even knew what it meant'. If the reader does not know this, the narrator will not explain − that is left the social-historian reader of the novel. To this indeterminate standpoint it is 'no surprise' that the cook should mutiny, but the threat that 'things would get worse' brings the narration closer to the narrator again, for he alone sees the future; only to move away once more to the register of reported thought − this time with ironic overtones − with the concluding comment that 'things were threatening to take a dreadful turn for the worse'. Clearly the narrator does not feel that the historical scene which is to follow, the comic operetta of a revolution, is dreadful or that, in its externals, it is as weighty as that undercurrent of family decline which is moved forward in the coming chapters by the deaths of Lebrecht Kröger and the Consul himself. Without commenting openly, the narrator has made his position clear.

Mann's light touch in the narration comes from his readiness to use other narrative positions than his own and, more often than not, to leave the last word to the story. For the most part he holds back the narrative voice behind the directly and indirectly recorded opinions and thoughts of his characters, from whom he thereby strongly distances himself. He shows his hand − juxtaposing a telling detail, underlining the opulence of the Buddenbrooks' gifts in the opening section, pointing out the toll that age takes on Tony's looks (6,10), emphasising the empty religiosity of the Consul's entry in the family book (2,1) and, as in the above example too, by slight stylistic overstatement in recorded speech, or by contrasting style-registers — but the technique depends for its effectiveness on being used sparingly. Mann's use of authorial generalisations (cf. 5,5; 8,5) is so restricted that — in view of Tolstoy's predilection for the technique and the fact that *Renée Mauperin* positively swarms with authorial generalisations — Mann must have avoided them deliberately. The narrator is prepared to surrender authorial omniscience at times, merely suggesting for instance, that, while Thomas listens to Tony's sentimental outpourings about life, he is 'probably' thinking of Anna (4,10) and he is quite content to leave his reader outside the music-room no wiser than Thomas about exactly what kind of activity is filling the awesome pauses in the passionate flow of the duet inside. As we shall see, he leaves open the cause of Thomas's death. Omniscience is a role the narrator assumes and discards at will, in the interests not of verisimilitude but of concentration on his theme.

The result of these techniques is a carefully composed polyvalence of voices and a relentless insistence on the *theme* (rather than, for instance, milieu) which Mann is concerned to communicate. As Julius Petersen, in one of the best studies of Mann's narrative technique, remarks: 'the narrator does not speak only as observer, concerned with an exact description of his object, with "reality": rather he opens up a horizon of meaning and filters the events he narrates through his own perspective' (Petersen, 192). We may see this concern for deeper meaning in two scenes from the final sections of the novel.

After the death of his mother, Thomas must negotiate the sale of her house with the broker Sigismund Gosch, the dreamer, would-be intellectual and poet of this generation (9,4). In some ways it is a trivial scene, for the big event — the fact that the Buddenbrook house will go to the Hagenströms — is still to come. It is Mann's technique which turns this slight occasion into something more significant.

As Thomas and Gosch meet, their conversation runs initially through reported speech, with the narrator merely dropping an ironic comment that Gosch's financial arguments could be compared to poetry. He then shows us, from within, Gosch's effort to compose his features into harmony with his offer, only then to take the opposite position and tell the reader that even 'a child' could have seen through this 'hypocritical mask' behind which Gosch's 'innermost knavery' attempted to hide. Thomas asks for time to think the offer over and enquires after Gosch's health. Gosch's reply begins as reported speech, but soon loses itself in an inner monologue of great passion in which Gosch passes his whole life in review, raising all the themes with which Thomas's life is preoccupied – ambition and idealism, hope and will – but not articulating them to Thomas. Indeed, he holds these thoughts back from Thomas, regarding him as too successful and too insensitive to understand what he means. The tone is very similar to that in which Thomas himself on occasion addresses his less gifted business colleague Stephan Kistenmaker (5,3), and there is comedy as well as tragic irony in Gosch's failure to know Thomas as the reader knows him. Gosch does not see Thomas's pained reaction as Gosch assures him '"You are happy"': he – Gosch – is too busy thinking about the euphony of his sentence. It is the narrator's unseen hand which ties in the loose ends and turns the scene into a sombre foreshadowing of Thomas's last days, weighing aspiration and achievement, success and sensitivity, appearance and substance. All of this has been achieved without breaking the narrative distance from the characters, and without authorial generalisation. The actual conclusion of the scene, the striking of a deal on the sale, is a deliberate anticlimax: what matters is the level of truth which Mann has engineered.

It is appropriate to take a final example from Hanno's sections of the novel. They are, in terms of their inception, the 'oldest', closest to Mann's original plan for the novel, and one might imagine that aspects of the writing here, being closely autobiographical, might engage the writer's sympathies more immediately. Manifestly the account of Hanno's day at school involves a biting criticism, with which the narrator is in full sympathy, of the Prussianised school system Mann himself had undergone. The mixture of cruelty and subservience, pedantry and careerism, the depiction of group dynamics in the service of heartless authoritarianism — Hanno's observations have a force which the narrator does nothing to reduce. Hanno's own role in this section — which is to observe from the outside with hardly less sharpness than the narrator's — leaves no need for the narrator further to intervene. However, the narrator surrenders thereby neither his distance from Hanno nor his omniscience in these sections, as, for instance, his several references to the sexual problems associated with Hanno's age make plain. These are observations that Hanno would not pass on to the reader, but the narrator's interest in unmasking the school so overlap with Hanno's — he is in this scene so unusually interested in his object, 'reality' — that narrative distance, though present, is harder to trace as a separate element. A more neutral scene, such as that in which Hanno returns to Lübeck from his summer holidays at the seaside (10,3), more clearly shows how Mann's narrative intention goes beyond individual characters to a theme of which they are unaware.

The chapter opens with a rather stylised paragraph explaining the arrangements for holidays in the Buddenbrook family. 'For many a year now the Buddenbrooks had become unaccustomed to extensive summer journeys', and soon the reason for this prolix language becomes clear. Gerda ('the Senator's wife') and Thomas ('her husband') have disagreed about how to spend the summer — disagreed is almost too strong a word for a difference of opinion which is as little articulated as is Thomas's agreement, 'in a fairly taciturn manner', to the plans — and the language is over-formal to mirror that. In contrast, the next paragraph announces another perspective, naive and incautious:

Summer holidays at the sea! Could anyone, absolutely anyone, imagine what happiness that meant?

The informality and liveliness of this sentence in free indirect speech is soon revealed to be that of Hanno, although the narrator immediately suggests the limitation of this perspective —

Never could little Johann understand how one teacher or another could bring themselves at the end of the lesson to utter phrases, like for example: 'We will go on after the holidays at this point . . .'

— by the contrasting linguistic registers; nevertheless the narrator is content to allow Hanno the joys of the seaside. He suits his narration, in its delightful combination of precision and vagueness, to Hanno's mood, and takes up into his narration the precise terms of Hanno's joy at being away from school:

No, God be praised, none of those smooth worsted coats came out here, who championed the cause of the three-times table and grammar, no they didn't come out here, because it was pretty expensive here.

Through the highlighting of the casual phrase in Hanno's thoughts, again in free indirect speech ('pretty expensive'), the narrator asserts himself, showing the snobbery no less deeply rooted in Hanno's enjoyment of the seaside than the rebellion of sensitivity Hanno himself is aware of. It is Hanno's eyes that take in the scenery from his bedroom window, although the reader is not as indifferent as Hanno to the name of the ship arriving from Copenhagen: the reader knows that the ship is a part of the world Hanno is trying to escape from, that to focus on its beauty is to neglect its utility value. So Hanno's perspective is never dominant. He does not understand exactly who the guests are who come to Travemünde for the day, and with his ear for naturalistic detail the narrator is content to record Ida Jungmann's snobbish comment on them, 'Eintagsfliegen' (day-trippers). Hanno's perspective cannot understand the scandals and gossips which surround Consul Döhlmann, Senator Gieseke and the rest. We learn of them partly from the guests' own mouths and partly because the narrator fills in the details. But the simple pleasures of the beach — waving to the steamers, donkey-rides, being read to on a bench — are seen directly, without irony or distance. The narrator tries neither to side with an adult reader nor to identify with Hanno, he merely steps aside and lets Hanno do the seeing. When Thomas comes out to visit at week-ends, it is from Hanno alone that we learn of Thomas's 'critical and enquiring' scrutiny of him. We are not told how Thomas reads the situation; here, as so often in the novel, it is the reader's imagination that must fill the gap.

The narrator does not surrender omniscience in this scene. It constantly provides a frame for these beautiful weeks at the sea, never intrusive but always creating the overall perspective. The omniscience speaks unmistakably in two remarks which Hanno also hears, but understands differently. As he waves his handkerchief to the steamers, Hanno listens to

the way in which the little waves slapped against the stone blocks and the whole expanse roundabout was filled with this gentle and splendid ringing, which graciously addressed itself to little Johann and persuaded him to close his eyes in immense satisfaction.

These voices are associated in Hanno's mind with the peaceful and untroubled sleep that he enjoys at the sea, but for the reader they have a different message. The sentence shows us how the words move from the range of Hanno's cognition ('the little waves') through slightly strange juxtapositions of which he is not capable ('gentle and splendid') to a level of linguistic formality which suggests that by now Hanno is the victim rather than the perceiver of the sea's noises. The waves speak to him, as they will shortly speak to Thomas (10,6), of death, and this is the voice the reader hears, perhaps even connecting it to the 'great and thankful satisfaction' Thomas experiences as he reads Schopenhauer a few pages later (10,5). In the same way Hanno is called home for supper by Ida Jungmann in an old-fashioned and rather silly way — 'catch your death if you should want to sleep here'. The phrase is part of her normal language of nursery exhortation, with which the reader is familiar. (In the opening pages of the novel old Johann had severely rebuked Ida for the 'stupidity' and 'obscurantism' which she had been teaching Tony (1,1)). Mann's command of natural detail and realistic character-portrayal is perfect once again, but nevertheless the reader accepts the hint and understands Ida's remark as an indication of the morbidity of Hanno's love of the sea. The key signature of decadence and decline is announced again; the reader, unlike Hanno, cannot escape from it, even during the holidays.

For Hanno the weeks in Travemünde pass and the journey home begins, marked by Hanno's final adieu and the tips to the servants. As the carriage drives Hanno back to Lübeck, we look with him − sitting opposite a 'white-haired and bony' Ida Jungmann − at the waves and lighthouse. The narrator adds a touch of social observation, underlining the class differences which exist and to which Hanno returns: the barefooted children staring curiously at the coach. Ida reassures Hanno that he will be back next year, and it is explicitly from outside that we watch as Hanno's chin quivers and 'the tears well out from under his long lashes' − from Hanno's perspective, of course, the scene would swim through the tears, but the reader is being asked to see Hanno from another point of view here. We see from the outside how the sea and sun have changed Hanno's appearance and made him brown, but it is his own sinking feeling that tells us how misplaced would be any hope that he has become 'harder, more energetic, fresher and more resistant'. We recognise the origin of these terms in other people's vocabulary and value-systems, but stay with Hanno's thoughts until the carriage reaches the ferry and then the town, where Thomas greets them. By then the narrator is back in charge, bringing along the three dreadful Buddenbrook sisters to cross-examine Hanno, and reporting omnisciently on Hanno's 'secret tears'.

The real point of the chapter is still to come. Perhaps it is only at the end of the chapter, if at all, as Tony reminisces with Hanno about the happiness of Travemünde and about her efforts to preserve it by taking home a jellyfish and catching the sparkle in its body (Hanno is bringing back the sand in his boots with a similar hope), that the reader is suddenly aware that the chapter just finishing is a repeat, a play-back of Tony's own return from Travemünde many years ago, after Grünlich had broken up her idyll with Morten (3,12). What she has brought with her from those days is little enough − half understood democratic phrases, a taste for honey − and perhaps in any case the memory and the jellyfish have lost their value and merely smell of 'rotten seaweed' (10,3). This judgement is an intellectual act left to the reader. Whichever way the reader decides, the parallels are there; line after line of the early chapter is echoed in Hanno's return.

The differences merely underline how far the family has sunk. There was no Uncle Weinschenk in the gaol by the Burgtor when Tony went by, just as Hanno does not have to wait outside the house for three huge wagons of Buddenbrook corn to pass before he returns home: times have changed for the worse, but the narrator shows his readers what Hanno never knows and Tony only intuitively suspects — that Hanno too is a 'link in a chain' — but that it is the chain of defeat and decline, and that the road to Lübeck is paved with a longer despair.

'Leitmotiv'

We mentioned the use of the symbolic 'Leitmotiv', the sea, which whispered to Hanno (as later to Thomas) of approaching death. In addition to the intellectual structure of the novel — its psychological and historical pursuit of the causes and manifestations of the family's decline — the novel is constructed 'musically', by the counterpoint of suggestions and hints, details and recurring symbols or leitmotifs. Mann himself was at pains to stress the musical element in its construction (to Grautoff, 26 November 1901) and he wanted readers to notice it. As has often been argued, Mann was neither unique in the use of the 'Leitmotiv', nor does Wagner — whose music Mann knew intimately and loved 'passionately' if not uncritically at the time of writing *Buddenbrooks* (XII,73) — provide the only source of the technique. Tolstoy and Zola both use recurring physical details in their novels to highlight important aspects of character or situation. Although Wagner and his techniques are usually thought of as being closer to the symbolists, with less affinities to realism — Mann reinforced this idea in his subsequent commentaries on *Buddenbrooks* by insisting that, while the 'Leitmotiv' was used purely 'mechanically' by the naturalists, he had used it 'symbolically' (XI,611) — in fact we note that Mann uses the device exclusively for its intellectual–psychological, analytical function and never in order merely to introduce mood or soft focus. The sea, honey, the house, blue shadows

under the eyes, Sesemi Weichbrodt's exhortation to suc-
cessive generations to 'be happy': whatever example one
takes, the motif's function is to show stages on the road to
decline or to give wider significance to individual experiences
and to show the interrelations between separate events − 'to
bring alive the constellation of forces which lies behind the
events' (Peacock, 21). While this illumination is often the
direct work of the narrator, at other times it is the characters
themselves who draw attention to the special significance particular objects or words hold for them, and so the use of
'Leitmotiv' becomes an integral part of the psychological
study of the Buddenbrooks' readiness to live by tokens: a
habit which is a central indicator of the weakening of their
will and grasp on reality. After all, it is Thomas who is minded
'to adopt as his favourite truth the saying that all human
activity has only symbolic meaning' (6,7). His attitude
towards his new house (7,6) − he identifies his own need for
an outer expression of success as a sign of weakness in himself
− is a clear example of a 'Leitmotiv' being recognised by the
characters themselves as a key to their own psychological
state.

Only once, with great irony, does a 'Leitmotiv' take on
independent action of its own: when Thomas dies from that
recurring symbol of his and Hanno's decadence, his bad
teeth. A merely naturalistically-minded reader would certainly echo the sentiments of Lübeck's citizens − 'From a
tooth? [. . .] Senator Buddenbrook had died from a tooth,
was the story in the town. But, for heaven's sake, you don't
die from *that*!' (10,9). Such a reader might well feel cheated
as the narrator passes from these reflections and takes refuge
again in the everyday, the piles of wreaths and palm-fronds
which are delivered at the house and which the newspapers
discuss at length: the cause of death is the more intriguing
problem. As penance for the indulgence in symbolism, Mann
gives Hanno a death very nearly straight out of the medical
encyclopaedia, quite uncluttered by 'Leitmotiv'. But the
function even of Thomas's death, for all its implausibility
(itself heightened by the naturalistic *details* of a meticulous

man dropping in a filthy street), is to push the reader back into a psychological enquiry into Thomas's state of mind, forcing the reader to consider the sequence of degeneration in the family and its continuation in Hanno. Even this technique is kept subservient to Mann's thematic concentration.

'Bilse and I'

We see therefore that Mann's achievement was to integrate into the thematic concern of his novel — its enquiry as to the 'egg' from which the 'sensitive late-comer' had hatched — a wide range of literary techniques. He not only drew on his immediate literary models, but went beyond them to find his personal style. It is appropriate at this point to see how Mann summarised his approach to literature, in the seemingly ephemeral essay of 1905/6 to which we briefly referred: 'Bilse and I' (X,11 – 22).

Mann's starting-point, we recall, had been to emphasise the difference between his text and the actual events of family and civic history from which it set out. Nevertheless, Mann dismisses the idea that the activity of writing consists of so-called invention, the creation of new characters, places and stories 'from nothing'. Instead, art depends on observation, it draws on reality for the raw material of the literary work. Mann locates the special skill of the writer, quoting as higher authority Turgenev, Goethe, Schiller and Shakespeare, in the power to invest with a life of its own that which has been observed, to give it soul ('Beseelung'). The writer achieves this by a process of total identification with his material, and by filling out his model with the problems and feelings of his own choice. Not surprisingly, therefore, Mann stresses the personal 'intuitive' quality of the knowledge of the world which the writer mediates. Since the writer apprehends reality by the means of personal identification just described, his knowledge of the world, though concrete, cannot be called objective.

In this view Mann is on reasonably conventional idealist ground — his view of art shares none of the scientific claims which so many of the naturalist writers made − but to this conventional view he added a more modern dimension with the suggestion that art may reach objectivity, as it moves to analysis through linguistic and intellectual precision. Here, Mann suggests, lies the cause of the misunderstanding of the relationship between writer and reality of which he himself had been accused: namely, that the finished work of art possesses 'the appearance of a hostility of the writer to reality, an impression which is brought about by the fact that the mind which observes knows no considerateness and by the critical accuracy of expression'. This was the element of rigour that was to upset the uncle who acted as unwilling model for Christian Buddenbrook, and which caused an early critic to refer to the narrator's eyes as 'pistol barrels aimed at the world' (Korrodi, 90). It is this which Mann was to call naturalism (he should in fact have called it realism), the third stage in his novel's evolution.

Mann's reflections on the subject of observation are prominent in this essay. Many of his remarks fit naturally into that current of discussion launched in the mid-1850s by the realist movement in France. His argument contains many echoes of Flaubert, for instance of Flaubert's typically ambivalent comment (to Louise Collet, 6 July, 1852) '*The less you feel a thing the more you are likely to express it as it is* (as it is *always* in itself, in its essence, freed of all ephemeral contingent elements). But you have to have the ability to *make yourself feel it.*' He shares with the realists the view that observation implies a generally critical attitude to reality, and emphasises that art is concerned to pursue truth without presuppositions, relentless to unmask a reality which prefers to be treated with kid gloves and 'with sloppy phrases'.

So far these arguments serve only to emphasise how close Mann was to the realist movement, as if the skills of social observation and criticism which he brought to an already extant story had been his actual starting-point and inspiration. But this was not so, and 'Bilse and I' contains a psychological argument which reminds us of the starting-point of the novel in the attempt to find ethical justification for the concern with self. The essay throws into question the notion that socially critical observation is necessarily something of which the author should be proud. Mann confesses to his belief that observation is more than just an intellectual skill: it is part of the psychological make-up of the artist, an obsession which borders on 'martyrdom' for the artist, who retaliates against a world which has made him suffer by mercilessly observing and dissecting it. This argument (which is taken from Nietzsche) is further elaborated by Tonio Kröger, for whom literature is 'a gentle revenge on life' (VIII,33). Mann focuses on observation not as a means of cognition, but as a personal weakness of the artist, an affliction almost. Observation may reveal everything about the world, but it reveals everything about the author too. The writer who is aware of this weakness in himself conducts his socially critical observation of reality with ambiguous feelings.

This psychological perspective prepares the way for a statement of Thomas Mann's explicitly ethical concern in the essay. For reality, the process of being brought to light and articulated in literature is one of enlightenment. Mann firmly believes that art has an ethical justification with regard to reality, 'that evil and mute things can be redeemed and made good by the act of expressing them' – an admirable notion, although hardly calculated to mollify the resentful and far from mute Uncle Friedrich. But the ethical argument also applies to the artist. The pursuit of truth is an integral part, Mann argues, of the ruthless self-exposure of the artist. The reality which the artist so inconsiderately unmasks is a reality in which the artist, by identification with it, is inextricably involved and from which in any case he has no right to hold himself aloof. His analytical severity towards reality is part of a no less severe attitude towards himself. The truth about the world can only be found in truth about the self.

We have so far referred to these qualities of objectivity – apart from their ethical dimensions – in terms of their participation in the European movement which Mann loosely called 'naturalism'. But it is also important to notice their function in a more domestic literary context. The German tradition of the novel (and especially the popular provincial novel of Mann's day, part of the so-called 'Heimatkunst') was unused to analysis and intellectuality, and to the literary styles in which these attitudes are conveyed. Mood and feeling, identification with the characters (or total rejection of them) and ideological consensus – these were the novel's corner-stones. It was regarded as a 'German' style to write in what one reviewer called 'the synthetic, rather than analytical style' (Rossbacher, 215). A later critic has described the main stream of German fiction at this time as having reduced or altogether eliminated intellectual analysis, what he calls its 'cognitive function' (Müller-Seidel, 601). Mann's discovery in the European realist movement of a style to express his own distance from his social and intellectual milieu was, therefore, a crucial element in his emancipation from parochial, narrowly German attitudes. Questions of genre and novel-form involved more than simply formal considerations.

Summary

As we examined the text, suggesting the care with which Mann has included elements of historical and objective analysis and excluded prejudice and the parochial ideology of his milieu, we must not forget the qualities of the text in which such insights have been included. Much less often than Balzac does Mann allow himself to play the role of historian, and while it cannot surprise us to find how consistent are Mann's historical interests, we know from the experience of reading that the novel uses a discourse different from that of the historian, and aims at different effects. When Tony slams down her hymn book, or refuses the advances of a conveniently weeping clergyman, the narrative is clearly aiming at humour and, in the sub-text, a concrete (almost allegorical) demonstration of the will to live represented by Tony. In other words, the study of the family's decline, the uncovering of the mechanism of the family's will to life, remain central. Historical understanding may be mobilised in the service of this enquiry, but historical study never becomes an end in itself or forms a separate focus of theme or style.

This is evidently so even in the areas of more public history which we discussed in an earlier chapter. Just as the wars of 1864 and 1866 are seen in ironic juxtaposition to the nursery games of Hanno; just as the flood of peculiar pastors who, under the most authentic historical flag, make their entry to the Buddenbrook house do so largely to illuminate the weakened will to life of the Konsulin and to highlight ironically Tony's continued resilient attractiveness, the 1848 Revolution serves as grist to Mann's thematic concerns. That history offers material to the novelist, but does not write his script, is shown forcibly at the end of the episode, as the Consul's father-in-law, Lebrecht Kröger, dies. This scene is historically acceptable, the coincidence of revolution and the passing of a representative of the old generation is entirely appropriate, yet the narration makes clear that it is the narrator who controls his narrative. That harmless stone, thrown 'in honour of the revolution' by an unseen hand, soundlessly coming through the carriage window, brushing against Kröger's thick coat, arriving without sound or force, derives its direction and energy from the novelist, not from objective history, a novelist who shapes his plot, rounds off the action, meting out death and life as he thinks fit, using history but being neither its slave nor its echo.

We have seen therefore that the archaeology of the text is scarcely discernible on its surface, save in the preservation of the insights of the sensitive late-comer, or the outlook of the established majority of the Buddenbrooks – insights preserved and yet relativised, constantly shot through with intellectual awareness transcending both points of view. In pursuit of this level of understanding Mann uses a broad palette of techniques, and quite evidently composes each episode with a delicacy and skill infinitely remote from naturalist 'slice of life' techniques; suggesting once more that 'realism' in the broad period sense – a 'mode' and not just a style (Stern, *On Realism*, 79 – 80) – rather than naturalism, is the appropriate term to denote the novel's tenor. The novel's thirst for knowledge transcends more limited perspectives, but its sensitivity to knowledge gives the text a quality which only the most gifted naturalists could achieve. The evolution of the text has produced a synthesis of its modes of perception, and brought the elements of the text which might be thought of as distinct – the novel of disillusionment (Thomas Buddenbrook), the novel of Tony's marriages, the wider family chronicle and the inner story of Hanno's revulsion at the world – into the harmony of the finished text.

Chapter 8

The Buddenbrooks' decline: a typical story?

There are several reasons why this question should be addressed. It was, for a start, a perspective on his own work which Mann welcomed. Not only did his initial treatment of his material point in the direction of representativeness, understanding himself and his family as part of a larger whole: his social position in later life, especially during the Weimar Republic and as a prominent member of the intellectual community which had left Hitler's Germany, made him particularly anxious to achieve representative quality in his works. In the famous letter of 1936 to the University of Bonn (whose rector had just found him unworthy to hold an honorary degree in Hitler's Germany) Mann wrote that, even at a time when National Socialism had turned him into an exile and outsider, he was 'far sooner born to be a representative than a martyr'. It was an aspiration which lay behind his entire life and works.

This ambition coloured his own reading of *Buddenbrooks*. In 1901 when he was launching it onto the world, Mann asked Grautoff to portray the novel as being typical of the nation, although neither Mann nor his friend understood 'Germanness' to mean anything parochial or hostile to other cultures: it was the status of representativeness which Mann had in mind. In 1926, when *Buddenbrooks* had become widely known to a European public (he was to receive the Nobel Prize for Literature in 1929), Mann extended his idea of representativeness to include this new public. The lines from *The Magic Mountain* which we used to preface this book, although they relate to Hans Castorp's love for the music of Schubert, reflect Mann's response to the international echo which his own works had found. The 'love' for a work of art is significant; it says something about the person who experiences the love and, by extension, about the society and culture of Mann's readers: it suggests that the work of art is significant to the extent that it is representative. Mann went so far as to suggest that − in order to achieve such popularity − *Buddenbrooks* must contain representative elements of an 'inner biography of the European middle-classes' (XI,383). Vogt supports this view when he argues that the novel achieves representative status through its portrait, in Thomas Buddenbrook, of 'a personality-structure [. . .] common in bourgeois society and in the bourgeois family right up to the present' (Vogt, 69).

Such questions have taken on particular importance to literary historians since Georg Lukács rightly gave central prominence to the notion of the historically typical as a constituting element in realism. To assess a realist text, some assessment of its historical period is essential. This is not to claim that characters must be cast on the ocean of public history or rub shoulders with the great for their actions and interrelations to be seen as a microcosm of the historical process. Johann Buddenbrook only saw Napoleon, whose age he embodies; while Thomas Buddenbrook can have major historical importance even though the news of his election to the Lübeck Senate will hardly have reached neighbouring Hamburg. Fighting at Waterloo makes George Osborne (in *Vanity Fair*) no more realistic than a Becky Sharpe, whose battlefields are less public. Historical relevance does not transform characters in fiction into marionettes dancing to the banal rhythms of historiographical truism, transposing the established interpretations of an historical period into human form. Nevertheless, what Sartre has called the 'pressure of history' is shown mediated in the fictional world of interrelating characters, and the experience of reading realist fiction mediates, through the imaginatively grasped network of fictional characters, a supra-personal and ultimately historical understanding.

This concern for historical typicality in the European realist movement affected both character-drawing and plot-construction. Previous periods of literature, unconvinced of the power of economic and social conditioning and lacking

models of historical study which might bring new methods into literature, had stressed the virtue of universality, but the
writers of European realism and the critics who would classify
their work were drawn rather to a notion of typicality which
located the appeal of a work neither in eternal human experiences nor in the acceptance of universal ethical norms, the
notion that a character is 'good' or 'bad'. Paradoxically, the
realists created 'typical' characters by locating them in the
particular, by showing them as the product of particular en-
vironments and particular times. The technique is extensively
used by Balzac and is also central to the historical generalisations which Mann's direct models, the Goncourt brothers, so
often employ. They write, for instance, of Renée's suitor:
'Denoisel was a Parisian, or rather: he was *the* Parisian',
clearly assuming that this objective form of characterisation
makes the figure more familiar to the reader than a subjective
account of his moods and attitudes. The characters in their
novel are shaped by environment and period so completely
that they are able to epitomise and represent their age.

Since the issue of typicality is, ultimately, unverifiable —
save as a conscious intention behind a literary method — it is
unlikely that we can find one single answer to the particular
question we raised as to the representative status of the Buddenbrooks' decline. Neither the readers of today nor Mann's
actual public form a group with a homogenous experience or
interpretation of history. In the next section we shall look
briefly at the range of contradictory aesthetic judgements
passed on the novel at the time of its appearance; there was no
more unanimity in reviewers' opinions on the representativeness of the story, although it was generally felt that the novel
intended to portray the story of the Buddenbrooks' decline 'as
a typical case' (Lorenz, 149). One reviewer discussed the novel
in the context of the news, which she had 'not exactly by
chance' read recently, of the collapse of three long-established
banks. Her comment that this was no coincidence and that
these bank-collapses showed the danger of 'degeneration'
makes clear that she regarded the novel as typical of certain
social circumstance (Neményi, 377). Other critics strongly

rejected this claim. These early discussions (and many that have followed them) make clear that the issue of representativeness has two principal aspects. The first relates to the techniques of characterisation to which we referred above, the use of specific objective norms for interpreting human behaviour such as Mann learned from the Goncourts and employed, for instance, in his creation of Morten as a typified portrait of the revolutionary student generation − although Mann, as narrator, refrains from pointing out the typicalness of the figure. The other is a question of the extent to which the particular reading of history behind this technique corresponds to the understanding of history in the mind of the reader. This implies not just a method: it implies a judgement of historical facts, a matter of ideology.

There can be little doubt that, at an objective level, the fate of the Buddenbrook family is not characteristic of their class in this period of history. These years saw a continued ascendancy of the patrician bourgeoisie, and although new subgroupings were emerging the main stream of the traditional bourgeoisie adapted successfully to the new climate. In this sense, another novel of Lübeck business life, published some ten years after *Buddenbrooks* − Ida Boy-Ed's *Ein königlicher Kaufmann* (A royal merchant) (1910) − more closely corresponded to the actual historical situation. In this novel, a Lübeck businessman hero, like Thomas a Senator and a 'fanatic of work', makes an enormous success of his business by means of overseas speculation, industrial investments and the like. These forms of economic activity became typical for the Lübeck bourgeoisie. It was clear from many reviewers' responses to Boy-Ed's novel that it more closely corresponded to their view of a representative picture of Lübeck society than *Buddenbrooks* − one reviewer remarked that the 'setting sun' of Mann's novel had been very properly countered by the 'rising sun' of Boy-Ed's work (Zimmermann, 346). When, therefore, Thomas retreats into pedantry and traditionalism he is hardly moving in the direction regarded as typical of his business colleagues or of his class. Indeed it would be accurate to say that Mann uses the historical norm every time this points a downward path for the Buddenbrooks (1848, the rivalry of Hamburg, isolation from the Customs Union), but departs from this norm if it seems to augur better times.

A particular example of this is the Austrian war of 1866, which in fact brought great economic advantage to Lübeck in the wake of the increasing economic ascendancy of Prussia, in contrast to Frankfurt which, by siding with Austria, lost out badly. It is quite contrary to historical trends that the war should inflict another blow on the Buddenbrooks' financial fortunes – the loss of twenty thousand thaler caused by the bankruptcy of a Frankfurt company. The scene is well documented, but it can hardly be described as historically typical. It serves instead as a reminder of the novel's insistence on its own theme of decline, and on motivating externally an inner process of decay. That, as for instance the work of Pierre-Paul Sagave has repeatedly shown, the novel is absolutely scrupulous in its recording of the details of social and economic history (and this fact is relevant to our classification of the novel's method) does not mean that it has to be following the main current of its age. The question is whether this 'failure' diminishes the realism of the novel.

In the German Democratic Republic the eminent historian Jürgen Kuczynski appeared to throw into disarray the conventional wisdom on the novel by claiming that its plot of the downfall of a family within an ascendant class was 'absolutely uncharacteristic'. For critics in Lukács' tradition – in particular for Inge Diersen – this was a serious charge, threatening the canonical authority which the text possessed, by virtue of its historical truth, over and against the 'avant-garde' writers such as Kafka. Lukács himself had not seen the theme of decline in *Buddenbrooks* in terms of a diagnosis of the demise of a whole class, but rather as part of a cycle of decline and regeneration *within* a class, with Buddenbrooks taking over where Ratenkamps left off and Hagenströms taking over the mantle of the Buddenbrooks – a process indicated by the shifting ownership of the Buddenbrooks' house. This interpretation leaves open the question as to whether or not

Mann's novel is making a claim about the general decline of a class (the bourgeoisie), or a sub-group (traditional middle classes, 'Bürgertum') within that class – an issue of considerable importance not only in the interpretation of nineteenth-century history but also in the evaluation of Mann's status as a progressive writer of 'bourgeois realism' (to use Lukács' phrase). The debates which this issue has raised suggest that it is more useful to define realism in terms of its methodology, broadly understood, than in terms of the actual historical insights which it may reach. We have seen Mann's method clearly in his constant preference for historical and psychological interpretation of events: even within his historical generalisations, however, a *method* can be seen at work which it is proper to call realist, however we choose to evaluate his conclusions.

We see this most clearly when we consider a once current interpretation of the novel's historical message which emphasises the decline of the Buddenbrooks as a counterpart to the ascendancy of the Hagenströms. Such interpretations can be found both at the time of the novel's publication (even, as we shall see, before its publication) and in the work of critics at various times up to the early 1930s.

Cultural pessimism at the end of the nineteenth century with its suspicion of the forces of change inside Germany made it possible for many German intellectuals to identify the nationalist cause with the values represented by the traditional elements in German society, to equate the modern phenomenon of the 'Bourgeois' (in Sombart's sense: the parvenu new bourgeoisie) with the forces of civilisation which had risen up in war against Germany and which should therefore be resisted as the enemy within, and to see the Jew as an example of these forces of unwelcome modernity. The resentment that Tony feels at Hagenström's rise to prominence, the fact that Hagenström marries into a Jewish family and appears to be unscrupulous, offered ammunition to these ideologists at the time of *Buddenbrooks*' publication. An early reviewer was not alone in seeing the novel as a lament at the house and heritage of the Buddenbrooks falling to the 'despised Hagenströms' (Schönhoff, n.p.). Ten years later when, much to most people's surprise, Mann briefly espoused the cause of German nationalism and his essay 'Thoughts in Time of War' was being read by a public whose chauvinism was raked up by Sombart's pamphlet 'Traders and Heroes', which contrasted the ethically responsible, 'heroic' German businessman and the materialistic, Westernised, 'Jewish' trading mentality, such factors certainly encouraged people to read back into *Buddenbrooks* historical resentment of this kind.

An important reason why such interpretations were made lay in the existence of a literary tradition to which they were appropriate. A popular part of the German tradition of the novel was the 'Kaufmannsroman' (novel of commercial life), represented by Gustav Freytag's *Soll und Haben* (Debit and Credit) (1855), a novel once very widely read and certainly known to Thomas Mann. The plot of this novel was built up on the contrast between the careers of the over-virtuous German hero and a former Jewish friend who comes to possess all the negative stereotypes of the Jew that are familiar from anti-semitic literature. These negative aspects are associated with the business methods that the character adopts. Readers schooled on such books might well tend to see the relationship between Buddenbrooks and Hagenströms in a similar way. It is also noticeable that the Scandinavian family novel on which, at an early stage of *Buddenbrooks*' evolution, Mann modelled his work, articulated great resentment about the declining morality of commercial life, and once more the target was the new bourgeoisie, the Hagenströms' Scandinavian equivalents.

Such resentment − and the historical perspective on which it was based − belonged to the parochialism of the genre which Mann overcame. It was also part of the heritage of Mann's own family with which he so decisively broke in the writing of the novel. One needs only to compare Mann's text with one of its sources − Julia Mann's stories of Hagenström's historical model, Fehling by name − to realise how strongly the novel moved away from evaluative attitudes towards a 'parvenu' class. Julia's attitudes towards Fehling (her letter speaks of his 'dishonesty and duplicity') are relativised by being transferred to Tony and portrayed in a distanced way as part of her doomed rearguard action to save the family.

When we look at the role Hagenström actually plays in the novel, we see two characteristic features of Mann's method: first that Hagenström's role in society is constantly seen from Thomas Buddenbrook's own perspective, whether as an artificial stimulus to unwonted activity (as in the Pöppenrade harvest episode, where Thomas *emulates* Hagenström), or (as in the Senate election) as part of what Thomas recognises to be token rivalry. In other words, the Hagenström theme, like everything else, is rigorously subordinated to the main thematic preoccupation of the novel. Secondly, we notice that, as Lukács observed, the Hagenströms participate in a pattern of behaviour recognisably associated with the traditional middle classes. There is a progressive development even in the Hagenström family. A generation which shows rude health and business vigour is succeeded by one with signs of refinement, intellectuality and perhaps even decline.

We should recognise, therefore, that the indeterminacy of the novel's historical perspectives − which comes from Mann's insistence on the theme of decline − should not be confused with indifference to intolerant and prejudiced readings. Any understanding of the novel's achievement must include the recognition that it operates by *analysis*, by juxtaposition and by distancing. It may well be, as Mann remarked in 1918, that he took over elements of the 'sociological' attitudes of his milieu 'half consciously' into the novel: once within the orbit of the novel, however, such unconscious elements were brought to the light, articulated and rendered material for scrutiny. It is for this literary method rather than for its historical generalisation that the novel continues to lay claim to our attention.

Chapter 9

Literary background and reading public

We have seen how the novel moved from dream to substance, from plan to realisation, and from complex and varied intentions — ethical, intellectual and aesthetic — to a narrative texture which embodies them. In this process Mann departed from 'history', both as some of his contemporaries interpreted it and as it is understood today, yet evolved a method which enabled him to stay close to it. In this section we relate this undertaking to the intellectual and literary climate of Mann's day, hoping to emphasise the personal nature of Mann's achievement, wrought against the considerable complexity of the literary scene in which he was writing.

As an ambitious writer Thomas Mann of course knew the literary fashions of the time well, and used them as models in some of his earliest works. At the same time, however, he knew both the major intellectual sources behind the fashions (for instance, Nietzsche) and the canonical literature which stood outside the changing trends of the moment. In the sense that *Buddenbrooks* drew on many models, it was dependent on given literary forms; while, as we saw, it also fulfilled a significant non-literary function in Mann's personal development. The success of such a work in part depends on the co-extensiveness of its personal function and its ability to mobilise the literary conventions of the day in furthering the personal aims of the individual work.

In the second half of the nineteenth century Germany had failed to produce a tradition of socially analytical realistic works such as existed in other European countries. This literary historical fact, commented upon then and since, was related to the wider phenomenon of cultural pessimism. In its hostility to urbanisation (from which naturalism drew so many of its themes) and in its rejection of the analytical techniques of the exact sciences (which naturalism applied to literature), cultural pessimism encouraged the survival in Germany of cultural and literary traditions more focused on the inner rather than the outside world, a literature which encouraged what Lukács usefully described as 'romantic anti-capitalism'.

So it was that Mann could describe *Buddenbrooks*, even though it appeared more than twenty years after Zola had published his first major novels, as 'the only naturalist novel in Germany'. The naturalist movement itself arrived late in Germany, achieving its significant literary fruits with the dramas of Gerhart Hauptmann in the early 1890s, and it was remarkably short-lived. No sooner had naturalist theories (for instance the emphasis on milieu and some kind of scientific approach to human behaviour) become accepted, than the counter-movements long since established in France undermined naturalism's position. In any case, many of the figures championed by the German naturalists (Ibsen and Strindberg for instance) had themselves moved on to different styles and different themes, exploring what Strindberg called 'the richness of the soul-complex' rather than overtly social themes. There was an obvious parallel between literature's discomfiture with its fixation on the large-scale external issues of society (the urban milieu, man's public and social behaviour, the writer as associate of the sociologists) and cultural pessimism's fear that traditional values were under threat in society. This is not to argue that all movements against naturalism shared the radical conservatism of cultural pessimism (although many did), but it is important to remember that the failure of naturalism to become established in Germany had a socio-political dimension.

The 1890s in German literary life may be summarised, in the phrase which Hermann Bahr coined in 1892, as 'the overcoming of Naturalism'. The writing of these years shows a concern for individual feelings, for *intérieurs d'âme*, for the autonomy of artistic activity, for language as medium rather than instrument, for the unknown rather than the known in man. Bahr gave this summary of the situation: '*états de choses*, endless objects — people are thoroughly sick of those; there is a renewed longing for states of soul [Seelenzustände], *états d'âme*' (Bahr, 55). The mood of the time was similar to that diagnosed in England much later (where a naturalist tradition was more firmly established) by Virginia Woolf in her famous essay 'Mr Bennett and Mrs Brown'. Here she suggests that the reality of life has been lost sight of behind a concern for the mere externals of life, the 'calico and the cancer'. What people really are hides beneath the surface of their social being, the human essence of life having fled from the areas in which naturalism had searched for it. In his preface to *Le Disciple* Paul Bourget, a writer whom Bahr did much to popularise in Germany, had written evocatively of the elusive human essence, 'this ocean of mystery which breaks on our shore, which we can see before us in its reality, but for which we have neither ship nor sail'. To set sail on this ocean, Bahr looked for the emergence of a literature of the 'nerves' rather than the intellect, and for a psychology freed from positivistic science and sensitive to inner states. A greater contrast to naturalism could hardly be imagined.

It is easy to see that aspects of Mann's work up to and including *Buddenbrooks* relate to the various currents towards and away from naturalism. We can find much evidence of Mann's relations with the naturalist movement of the 1890s, from his acting in a German premiere of Ibsen's *The Wild Duck* to his publishing in M. G. Conrad's *Die Gesellschaft* and then with the publisher who had championed naturalism, Samuel Fischer. Mann's collaboration in the periodical *Das zwanzigste Jahrhundert* brought him close to cultural pessimism, though this work did nothing to shake Mann's positive attitude towards his Jewish fellow-citizens, and merely served as a stepping-stone to journalistic experience. As we saw, some reviewers mistakenly viewed the Hagenström theme as evidence of Mann's sympathy for the movement. At the same time, Mann's closeness to the movement away from naturalism can be seen in the dedication of his first published work to Hermann Bahr, in the use in *Buddenbrooks* of a language of the 'nerves' — indeed, without this perspective much of Thomas's experiences would have escaped us; as the narrator comments: 'Our wishes and activities are the product of certain needs of our nerves which are hard to define in words (7,5) – and in Mann's – albeit critical – passion for the music of Richard Wagner, spiritual father to the symbolists. None of these elements breaks with the 'naturalism' which Mann with some justification claimed for his novel; still less, as the novel's evolution suggests, passing as it did from introspection to 'naturalism', did Mann's participation in these movements merely follow the chronology of literary movements. Just as every historical moment contains a multitude of different historical movements, some ascendant, others in eclipse, echoes of the past and anticipations of the future, so the literary scene that Mann experienced, like the language and works which are its expression, demonstrates what Ernst Bloch called the 'Ungleichzeitigkeit' of historical progress, by which he meant the simultaneous co-existence of heterogenous elements in each moment of history, where changes in society and in the ideological superstructure take place at different speeds, with transitions even where there are frontiers between the old and the new, where the past may be 'overcome' but continues to exist and to be effective.

If the intellectual climate in which *Buddenbrooks* was composed was anything but homogenous, it is no less evident that Mann responded to the literary scene in a differentiated and personal way. A figure such as Paul Bourget, who was very influential in the 1890s, had much to offer him: psychological interest in the dilettante, exploration of the origins of artistic sensibility, a view of the divided self. These themes appealed to Mann for personal reasons, as an account of the condition of the artist, that profession to which he was aspiring. Other themes of Bourget's interested him less (for instance his attention to erotic matters) and Mann ignored them. His other reading, from Goethe and Heine to Nietzsche, from Tolstoy to the Goncourts, set up counter-balances to the fleeting influences of fashion. Where the literature he encountered did not offer answers to the actual situations Mann confronted and with which his works wished to deal, he left them alone. As we have seen, it was the achievement of *Buddenbrooks* to reach a balance between the retreat into introspection and the insistence on the reality of society and on the validity of intellectual-analytical criteria. Mann's success is to have achieved this balance, and — what is more remarkable — under the all-but unruffled surface of the realist novel, so much of which is devoted to the prosaic round of work, marriage and money, to have included the ocean of the unknowable lapping against the shore of an all-too-familiar provincial milieu. This balance is the achievement of the text: we may trace its separate elements in the literary climate of the day, but we shall not find there the balance itself.

Something of the complexity of the literary climate in which *Buddenbrooks* was composed can be seen in a brief survey of the variety of critical responses which the novel evoked at the time of its first appearance. The lack of unity in the literary climate of Mann's day, which is reflected in the novel's reception, points to Mann's literary technique as a deliberate selection from conflicting tendencies of the time, suggesting that we should see literary history not as a set menu with a fixed order of courses, as if it were literary history that made *Buddenbrooks* turn out as a naturalist novel, but rather as a series of *plats du jour* from which the writer chooses.

It would be unusual, of course, if the critical reception of Mann's novel had been unanimous. The commercialisation of fiction which we experience in our own age has so 'homogenised' literature as commodity that different opinions on a work become merely 'controversial', and we are perhaps less used to genuinely divergent readings of literary works. Although publishers in 1901 knew a surprising amount about selling novels (reviewers repeatedly commented that Mann's novel was less well marketed than Gustav Frenssen's highly conventional *Jörn Uhl*, which everyone read then and no-one reads now), the wide range of opinions on Mann's novel had a deeper cause than a poorly targeted sales campaign. The diversity was also greater than can be explained simply by the ideological debates we referred to earlier as to whether or not the novel's plot was 'representative'. The novel, combining as it did elements of realism with elements of anti-naturalism, constantly fell between the expectations of reviewers. So one reviewer complained of the novel's 'Naturalism, without hope and without ideas' (Stockmann, 565), while another, recognising that the novel was naturalist in its use of 'an almost scientific method of observation', praised it for exploring – unlike 'Zola and some German imitators' – human themes of the kind for which Hermann Bahr had argued: namely 'the essence of man' (Eloesser, 1288). One reviewer complained of the excess of content in the novel (too much 'calico'), over-meticulous detail about the social and economic life of a not particularly remarkable family (Lorenz, 149ff): another complained of the opposite tendency, alleging that the actualities of the Buddenbrooks, 'the life and activity in the store-rooms, comptoirs, in the harbour and at the quay-side' were under-represented (Hart, 104). Mann's characterisation, too, was judged from incompatible standpoints. For one reviewer the characters were 'tangibly alive' (Meerheimb, 217); for another they were 'like so many Naturalist figures, really only there because of the milieu' (Krüger, 20). These were not differences of personal taste: they were reflections of a divided literary climate. One reviewer could say that 'the completely modern feature' of *Buddenbrooks* lay in the fact that the driving force behind characters and events came 'not from the outside, but from the inside of what is described ' (Heine), while another review claimed that the novel completely left out the real forces leading to the decline of the Buddenbrooks (Lorenz, 150) – meaning presumably that the novel did not concern itself with interesting behaviour outside the stable worlds of family salon and business. There was little understanding for the fact that Mann wished to show both the causes and the social manifestations of sensitive inwardness: that neither social issues nor inwardness on their own were his theme.

Mann had found his artistic method in this contradictory

climate, but he was still far from having a realistic view of his public. This emerged in his understandable, but rather naive, request to his friend Otto Grautoff to review the novel in such a way as to assure for it a good reception among readers in Lübeck. This ambition and the form it took (at Mann's behest Grautoff's review called *Buddenbrooks* 'a genuinely German novel') were not only less than true to the spirit of the novel with its transcendence of narrow, parochial values; they also showed a fair misreading of the actual public which his novel might have. How could the Lübeck background which he knew to be profoundly 'unliterary' suddenly provide him with his readers? There was only one possible answer to the fundamental question posed by one reviewer: 'Is the essential point of this novel of commercial life to be found in a few sugar sticks [i.e. in the material circumstances of the Buddenbrooks' life, HMR], or in a few human minds?' (Korrodi, 90). This question points to a split in Mann's reading public still more serious than that between naturalists and anti-naturalists. The split between the actual reading public for quality literature and the public Mann seemed to aim at (the traditional middle classes about whom he wrote) was a well-known feature of the German literary scene. As one reviewer of *Buddenbrooks* commented: it was 'irrelevant to the German public if a novel is written well or badly' (Eloesser, 1281) – such matters were for the specialised readers of literature. If *Buddenbrooks* has achieved, in the course of this century, a readership that is both popular and specialised, this cannot disguise the fact that in its day the novel was liable to be understood only by the specialist group. Mann might have learned from the example of his great predecessor, Theodor Fontane, who, despite writing extensively on themes taken from and – he presumed – appealing to a particular class (the landed and minor aristocracy of Prussia), was actually read by a radically different public. In an entertaining poem written on the occasion of a seventy-fifth birthday marked by the complete absence of tributes from the aristocracy amongst whom he had found so much of his material, Fontane accepted the homage of what he

learned to be his actual readers, the urban Jewish intelligent-
sia (Bramsted, 267f). His experience held a lesson which
Mann, hoping for an appreciative reading public in Lübeck,
was slow to learn.

The reception of *Buddenbrooks* showed, therefore, that the
reading-public was divided in ideology, in aesthetic taste and
in its appreciation of literature. These divisions made it vir-
tually impossible for all but a few critics to see that Mann had
managed to combine the elements of a contradictory literary
scene and to form something new out of them. While these
few far-sighted reviewers included the poet Rilke, it was the
critic of the *Berliner Tageblatt*, Samuel Lublinski, who pro-
nounced the words on *Buddenbrooks* of which Mann was
subsequently most appreciative, saying of the novel: 'It will
grow with time and be read by many generations to come'
(1902 review in Vogt, 147f). As the novel's first appearance
grew more distant in time − also as critics found in short
stories such as 'Tonio Kröger' a further key to Mann's views
on art − it was easier to take a wider view of the novel's relationship to its age. So a critic perceptively characterised the
work in 1907 as 'Naturalism on the way to becoming symbolic' (Bertram, 79), but it was once again Lublinski who
gave the most illuminating account of the novel by referring
it to the particular situation of the literary-historical age in
which it was written. His major work of literary sociology,
Die Bilanz der Moderne (The balance-sheet of the modern
movement, 1904), is a magnificent attempt to summarise the
period from 1890 and includes a range of insights beautifully
attuned to *Buddenbrooks*. A particular example − we have
not the space to give a full account of Lublinski's approach
− is his observation that it is paradoxically the scientific
method of Social Darwinism which has revealed the symbolic
dimensions to life, showing the importance of everyday life to
be as a cloak for that struggle for existence which is the true
centre of human experience. As we saw, it was precisely that
combination of analytical insight into reality (Hanno's vision
of the play-acting of the business round) and a readiness to
invest objects with deeper significance which characterises

Buddenbrooks. Lublinski's skill is to show this method embedded in its age. Indeed he understands the novel as a supremely skilled balancing act, made necessary by an age deeply divided: between 'ecstasy and exactness', science and personal feeling, analysis and intuition. His reading of *Buddenbrooks* is rewarding because it shows how the conflicting tendencies of the time are, in their contradictoriness, nevertheless harnessed to the narrative purposes of the novel. The mood of the novel, he argues, lives only between the lines, and

can be revealed only to a sensitive and very patient reader. For Thomas Mann devotes himself to a strictly naturalistic objectivity and almost never offers colour and lyricism, but clear and cold lines which he draws with firm and delicate hand, so that they cannot be blurred. This is part of the intellectual and manly stance of a young man who, in proud modesty, clenches his teeth and stands quietly as swords and spears pierce his body. This attitude matches the disposition of the novel's characters and that of its principal hero, the Consul and Senator Thomas Buddenbrook [. . .] The young poet reveals his own sympathies only by means of a melancholy irony, an armour which a reader of souls soon penetrates. So it is surprising that people should often have dared to accuse him of coldness and mere artistry, and the only explanation can be that this first and unique Naturalist novel appeared at a time when everyone had long since been swept along by Neo-Romanticism and Symbolism and looked exclusively to mood to provide a drugged oblivion.   (Lublinski, 226)

This is a fine reading of the novel and of the function of its conflicting aspects. Mann's appreciation of Lublinski's sensitivity to the text is evident from this passage, since Mann takes from it not merely the claim that his own work is 'this first and unique Naturalist novel', but also picks up the image of the writer pierced by swords and spears to characterise the work and personality of Aschenbach in *Death in Venice* (VIII, 453) – a typical example of Mann's readiness to weave oblique autobiography into his works. What is especially fine in this view is the balance between Lublinski's understanding of Mann's personal involvement in the novel and his reading of the literary – historical circumstances in which it was written. He sees clearly the experience Mann shares with his age (suffering in the face of his inadequacy to live up to the new demands of life) and understands that Mann deliberately chose to hide his personal suffering behind a style that, in its cold-ness, appears to deny the suffering and to side with precisely that mechanistic spirit of the age under which Mann was suffering. Lublinski shows, in short, that Mann had found a way to adapt to his personal needs the styles which literary history placed before him. His view of Mann's work therefore goes much further than merely to point out that the novel uses naturalist techniques. Behind this use Lublinski sees personal and ethical intentions, and in the dilemma with which Mann's own experience confronted him Lublinski sees a reflection of an age's uncertainty about itself. His exciting challenge to read between the lines or, in Benjamin's phrase, 'against the grain', reaps rich rewards.

Chapter 10

Buddenbrooks and the 'crisis of the novel'

Hanno: 'I thought there was nothing more to come'   (8, 7)

We quoted earlier Mann's claim to have written a 'naturalist' novel. His use of this term was coloured by the circumstances of German literary history and by Samuel Lublinski's particular choice of words, and — while in European literary discussions the word 'realist' would have been more usual — we have seen that Mann's claim for his novel was amply justified. In its narrative technique, its analytical approach to social reality, its reliance on observation and documentation and its pragmatic commitment to reality *Buddenbrooks* meets the expectations of the realist movement in European fiction and brings them to artistic fruition.

Within the context of German literature *Buddenbrooks* occupies the place of a landmark, and its achievement is to have brought the German novel into line with the great tradition of European fiction. One novel cannot create an intellectual revolution on its own, but it can demonstrate the possibilities of the moment, and the work of Thomas Mann (and to an important extent that of his brother Heinrich also) brought new standards into German fiction. The break with provincialism was achieved while — as Eberhard Lämmert has shown — bringing together European styles and traditional German forms, notably the novel of education ('Bildungsroman'), integrating the new and progressive with positive elements of the national tradition. The notorious lack of continuity of German cultural life in this century, broken repeatedly by wars and revolutions, by Hitler's Reich and by division, has made this achievement less fruitful than it might have been, but even such discontinuity cannot diminish its stature.

The literary achievement of one generation cannot simply be copied by the next. However much they are admired, the forms and genres that are valid for one age cannot be adopted by the next without modification, and the more radical the breaks between generations, the greater these modifications will be. As a recent critic has observed, literary forms and genres are 'historically conditioned forms of communication and mediation' (Voßkamp, 27): it is their appropriateness to the quality of personal and social experience that causes them to rise and fall with the succeeding generations. We saw this in Mann's search for genre as he worked on *Buddenbrooks*. His search was anything but a shopping-trip to a treasure store of eternally valid forms of the novel, rather an attempt to find forms appropriate to the themes and attitudes his historical situation had given him.

Many aspects of the modern movement can be seen as an approach to Mann's central problem in *Buddenbrooks*: to portray individual characters within a society whose values increasingly contradict theirs. As society has become less personal and less stable than the world of the Buddenbrooks, so the techniques of the novelist have had to change. The individual techniques and attitudes which the nineteenth-century realist writers used in their art (for instance, documentary, reported speech, interest in history) have not lost their validity; what seems unattainable is the ensemble of formal techniques and attitudes, in short the genre itself. Mann's situation in twentieth-century literature and the reception of *Buddenbrooks* are, therefore, inseparable from what is loosely called the 'crisis of the novel'. Indeed we may argue that the passage of time has eroded precisely those elements in the work which we can now recognise as having constituted the genre of the nineteenth-century realist novel. We may list these variously as: a vision of totality, confidence in narrative detachment, and the commensurateness of private and public history.

It is one of the hallmarks of the realist novel that, like a genie emerging from the lamp, or like that process by which a zoom lens turns close-up into long-shot, a picture of totality was created out of the portrayal of individuals enmeshed in personal and social relations, a totality which transcended individual experience. In his famous remarks on art at the end of the classical period, Hegel had argued that the novel could not assume that each individual was the complete expression of his age and society — this had been the feature of the epic which gave it such luminous pre-eminence in the history of human culture. In an age of alienation and the division of labour Hegel had suggested that the novel, as the successor to the epic, had the task of portraying a different type of historical experience, in which the individual appears 'not as the independent, complete and at the same time individually living representative of this society itself, but only as a limited member of it'. The novel must reconstruct in the telling of its plot the lost totality of the ancient epic and is concerned not with the natural unfolding of character in the plot, but the conscious search and struggle for self-realisation in the world. It was the achievement of realism, perhaps its purpose too, to give artistic form to this search for meaning, to demonstrate that it is possible to be a St Teresa in Middlemarch, a Caesar by the Baltic; to prove through the writing of fiction that 'Yvetot is worth Constantinople' (Flaubert), or that (in Fontane's example) a single drop of pond water is as intensely full of the totality of life as an heroic event such as Columbus discovering America. In this way the realists expressed their confidence in being able to enfold within their stories the totality of life which idealist philosophy had shown to be under threat. *Buddenbrooks* participates in this confidence, in part in the skill with which it sees ideas clothed in events. J. P. Stern refers to Thomas's death, for instance, as the 'consummation of its [the novel's] events and ideas alike' (1976,423): the identity of idea and event being the novelist's achievement. Clear too is Mann's faith in the novel to create that lesser totality, between the individual character and the historical movement. It was, after all, the skill in using individual characters to represent distinct periods of historical development that had first attracted Mann to *Renée*

Mauperin. This is a lesser form of totality, for it may be that what history gives to a character is precisely fragmentation and lack of rounded totality. So, for instance, Henri Mauperin was described as being marked by 'this important feature of the second half of the nineteenth century'; yet this was a description of an unnatural combination of characteristics, namely that of youth and coldness. Even such portrayals, however, presupposed the ability of the novel to summarise historical totality within individual characters, a confidence which we saw also in *Buddenbrooks*.

Such linking of subject and world, the creation of totality, is the achievement of the novel's narrator. If 'history', as Hegel argued, 'by itself' no longer created individuals who in themselves enshrined either the full totality of man's being or even the limited totality of the historical moment, then the novelist must create these for himself. Since the intention of realism is to restore totality as a feature of reality, rather than to present it as a personal vision of the artist's, the realist novel seldom personalises the act of narration. This is not to diminish the personal nature of the narrative achievement, for, as Adorno remarked in an important commentary on 'The Position of the Narrator in the Contemporary Novel' (1954), 'the subjectivity of the narrator is preserved in the power with which the illusion of reality is produced'. As we saw, this accurately denotes the techniques used in the narration of *Buddenbrooks*. Mann shares with realism the reluctance to locate sense only within subjective experience. His personal narrative stance achieves objectivity by being multi-personal, providing a shifting series of viewpoints, establishing sense and meaning in different places and in ways different from those suspected by the characters. Its mixture of identification and distance, empathy and analysis, consensus and outsider status is characteristic of the traditional realist novel.

It is a truism of literary history that these, the constitutive elements of Mann's novel, are precisely those features which the so-called 'crisis of the novel' has made problematic. Totality seems inaccessible to most novelists, and it is to make excessive demands on the novel that its knowledge should make sense of the world. Modernist writing, 'the one art that responds to the scenario of our chaos' as Malcolm Bradbury and James McFarlane described it in their recent volume, has no longer any confidence that it can achieve a totality which the world does not yield, and it sees no chance to create within itself a meaning which is more than private, which might reach out and signify the meaningfulness of the world. In an age of anonymous trusts and cartels, of mass-killing and of institutionalised inhumanity, the modern novelist seems unwilling to commit his work to public statement or to bring together private and public world as his nineteenth-century predecessors had done. His own function being so radically changed, the narrator figure takes on the task of questioning the narrative which in the traditional novel it was his subjective achievement to have created. As Adorno pointed out, the modern novel is characterised by the writer's 'committed stance against the lie of the presentation [of reality], in fact against the narrator himself'. Hence the proliferation of prose forms in which the narrative stance is either parodied or constantly reflected upon, or the fiction is created (in documentary writing) that narration is negated altogether.

It is understandable that these sweeping changes in the form and presuppositions of the novel should have had a considerable influence on the reception of a novel which, like *Buddenbrooks*, had brought the traditional skills of the genre to a late flowering. Whether one sees these changes as blight or blesssing, whether they represent a shift of taste or a change in the superstructure responding to change in the economic base, they have created a situation in which the literary form of *Buddenbrooks* is unlikely to provide a model for those writers who, like Mann himself at the turn of the century, endeavour to find the forms most appropriate to their historical situation.

In Germany, although Mann remained at the forefront of literary life for some fifty years after the appearance of his first novel, his own works showed that it was not sufficient to rest on the formal achievements of *Buddenbrooks*. His second major novel, *The Magic Mountain*, takes its place with Alfred Döblin's *Berlin Alexanderplatz* and Robert Musil's *The Man Without Qualities* as one of the seminal works of formal innovation, while *Doctor Faustus* is a magnificent exploitation, for the purpose of the historical interpretation of Germany's situation in this century, of the breaks in narrative certainty. The achievements of *Buddenbrooks* were not forgotten by critics, and still less by Mann's enormous popular following, but they were not emulated. When writers in western Germany tried to reconstruct a literature from the ruins of the Third Reich, they naturally turned to the models offered by writers and genres disapproved of by the National Socialists (for instance, the form of novel created by Döblin). It was less likely that they would orientate themselves towards the nineteenth-century realism of *Buddenbrooks*. Traditional German forms, such as the 'Bildungsroman', tend after 1945 to exhibit elements of parody. The major writers have not, for instance, generally used the traditional form of the family chronicle to tell the story of German history in this century, and one of the few major works written in this form – the late Heinrich Böll's *Billiards at half-past Nine* (1959) – departs radically from Mann's style, although Böll's admiration for *Buddenbrooks* was clear from his Frankfurt lectures of 1966.

Buddenbrooks' reception, as we have seen, soon reached more widely than Germany and increasingly, in recent years, it has been widely appreciated in the English-speaking world and enjoyed that kind of popular success which has accompanied its literary reputation in Germany. This has not always meant, however, that Mann's novel had received either so positive a response from critics or the tribute of imitation by his fellow-writers. Lawrence's dismissive attitude towards Mann, then taken over by the Leavis school, did not make it easy for *Buddenbrooks* to be assimilated into English culture as, for instance, Ibsen had been. Even in the 1960s D. J. Enright could suggest that on the basis of 'a nervous perusal of the opening pages of *Buddenbrooks'* English readers might find Mann 'wordy, philosophical, humourless, highly abstract and crammed with details'. Such insular judgements are fortunately less common now, so too is the tendency to see Mann as a pendant to Galsworthy. In France the continuance of the tradition of family chronicle novels gave Mann's work a stronger place in the critical debate, although it was in France that the consequences of Mann's political aberration in 1914 had the sharpest repercussions. In America, where Mann spent the years of the Second World War and wrote some illuminating commentaries on his own works, including the introduction to *Buddenbrooks* to which we have referred, it might still be difficult to trace much direct influence of this novel. Saul Bellow's obvious debt in *Herzog* to *The Magic Mountain* — an exciting transfer of Mann's central concerns to the American situation — only emphasises that the predominant influence on the early Bellow was not *Buddenbrooks* but the work of Franz Kafka.

Here we return to the pairing of names so significant for the reception of Mann in the last years. The work of Georg Lukács (so far we have mentioned only the essay on *Buddenbrooks*) is remarkable also for its apodictic attempt to set up evaluative models for literature in the post-modern period, categorising the possibilities of literature according to the models indicated in the title of the essay 'Franz Kafka or Thomas Mann?' (1954). We need not exaggerate the importance of this essay with its authoritarian alternative prescriptions, nor suggest that Mann is plausible as a socialist realist. Lukács was, nevertheless, recognising a need to harness the tradition of bourgeois realism to the task of the twentieth-century writer, trying to show that the 'crisis' of the novel and the experience of *Angst* and alienation so typical of our age do not have to mean the abandonment of the narrative techniques of realism. As a result, the essay neatly summarises a dilemma that is implicit in the literary historical situation of *Buddenbrooks*.

The choice Lukács sees for the contemporary novelist is between realism, even in the 'God-forsaken world' of the present age, and the avant-garde. Is fiction to provide, through the techniques of realism, a reflection of a distorted and alienated reality, Lukács asks; or should it abandon realism and the picture of totality which the realists communicated (the school-master's tone is typical of this piece), and provide instead a 'distorted reflection' of reality, bringing into its own narrative techniques the absence of totality, and showing the disjointed and broken nature of modern man's experience of life? That reality is alienated is accepted. The dehumanised world of the modern − whether or not one shares Lukács' understanding of this condition as a symptom of the highest form of capitalism − is certainly seen by the realist Thomas Mann. In Thomas Buddenbrook he gives a picture of the *Angst* which is the 'dominant existential condition' of the avant-garde. As a realist, Lukács argues, Mann understands this *Angst*, places it socially and psychologically, and uses his narrative to demystify it. Kafka on the other hand (we are told), as a representative of the avant-garde, lacks such a perspective. He identifies the essentially subjective, 'distorted' experience of *Angst* with reality itself, and discloses nothing of the objective world outside individual, subjective experience. So Kafka provides a distorted portrayal of reality, rather than a realistic portrayal of distortion. The realistic details scattered in his work do not provide, as they do for realist writers, 'the nodal points of individual or social life' but they are instead 'cryptic symbols of an unfathomable transcendence'.

Lukács' presentation of choice had limited validity. Only within the orthodox canon of socialist realism (and even there only for a limited time) did his dogmatic tone achieve a reorientation of literary models. In practice it has been the opposition to Lukács' argument by Brecht, Bloch, Anna Seghers and Adorno which has been the more influential. Certainly Lukács' essay is not the best way to make Thomas Mann's work attractive, for not only does that essay underrate the social-critical element in modernism; it judges realism far too narrowly, seeing the reader's role in an altogether too passive way, and underplays Mann's modernism of style as well as theme, 'the increase in consciousness portrayed and a corresponding increase in the consciousness of the portrayal' (Stern, 1976, p. 425). Nevertheless, Lukács' essay does underline, usefully, the 'perennial' mode of Mann's realism. It pin-points Mann's determination, even when tackling themes of great abstraction — as in *Doctor Faustus* — to create a framework of reference to the real. To situate, to place, to analyse — this endeavour which characterised Mann's approach to the subject of his own early life in *Buddenbrooks* remained central to his subsequent work. What we suggested was a particular achievement at a particular historical moment — the portrayal of the escape by Thomas Buddenbrook out of the conceptual world of business, and into the world of contemplation and art, a portrayal which shows both the attraction and the limitations of the means of escape and situates it socially and psychologically in its exact position in the society of his day — that achievement reflected the perennial concern of all Mann's works. His first novel is remarkable not merely for bringing the German novel into the twentieth century, or for representing a highpoint in the art of the realist novel; not merely for fusing national and European traditions of fiction, but for achieving at so early an age a maturity and authenticity of personal style which would reach through a life's work of great novels, of which, as Mann wryly remarked in later years, *Buddenbrooks* was 'probably' the best.

Suggestions for further reading

There is so much secondary literature on Thomas Mann that his own works start to look rather short in comparison. Nevertheless, if, having looked over this short introduction and read the novel, the reader's appetite has been whetted, there are some excellent essays and books that will take interests further.

The novel relates closely to the short stories of the period (see Chapter 1), especially those concerned with the problem of the relationship between art and life, and a natural starting-point for further reading would be these stories, especially perhaps 'Tonio Kröger', 'Tristan' and 'Death in Venice', or any of the short stories in *Little Herr Friedemann*. They illuminate Mann's novel, both by their similarities and by their differences, and they allow the reader to judge whether (as one critic rather sourly commented) *Buddenbrooks* was an example of what happened when a master of the short story tried his hand at a novel.

It is also very easy to find Thomas Mann's many comments on his novel. In German they are available in the useful series 'Dichter über ihre Dichtungen' (vol. 14, 1), ed. Hans Wysling. English translations exist of a few of the essays in which Mann expressed his opinions on his first novel. Mann's correspondence has also been translated, although unfortunately not the interesting and useful letters to Grautoff, which are quoted at various points in this text.

Biographical studies

Biographical information on Mann is best available in the first volume of the standard biography, Peter de Mendelssohn: *Der Zauberer. Das Leben des deutschen Schriftstellers Thomas Mann* (Frankfurt, 1975). Two excellent English biographies make much of this material still more widely available: Nigel Hamilton, *The Brothers Mann. The Lives of Heinrich and Thomas Mann 1871/1950 & 1875/1955* (London, 1978), and Richard Winston, *Thomas Mann: The Making of an Artist 1875/1911* (London, 1982). A very useful survey of Mann's life and works is given by Hans Bürgin and Hans-Otto Mayer, *Thomas Mann: Eine Chronik seines Lebens* (Frankfurt am Main, 1965). Those interested in the early notes and manuscripts for *Buddenbrooks* are recommended to consult the work by Paul Scherrer (which is listed in the standard bibliographies). The original letter which Julia Mann sent to her brother about their aunt, the model for Tony Buddenbrook, is readily available in: Julia Mann, 'Tante Elisabeth' (*Sinn und Form*, 15, 2/3 (1963), 482–96).

Critical studies

There is some excellent work on Mann in English. Erich Heller's study of Mann's work makes exciting reading (*The Ironic German: A Study of Thomas Mann*, 1958, reprinted 1979), as does the superb study by T. J. Reed (*Thomas Mann. The Uses of Tradition*, Oxford, 1974). An interesting collection of essays by different writers is that compiled by Henry Hatfield (*Thomas Mann. A Collection of Critical Essays*, Englewood Cliffs, 1964).

Out of the German studies of *Buddenbrooks* several works stand out as particularly useful. Peacock's account of the 'Leitmotiv' remains a classic. Lämmert's interpretation is a fine, concise account of the novel, concentrating on its relation to the German tradition. Petersen's work on narrative technique remains the best on this topic. Lehnert provides many interesting insights into the relationship between the early stories and *Buddenbrooks* and on the relationship between ideology and narrative structure. Pierre-Paul Sagave, who pioneered the study of the social and economic background of the novel, is always worth consulting for a view of the documentary accuracy of Mann's work. Frizen offers a detailed study of the place of Schopenhauer in Mann's work. Jochen Vogt's excellent and highly readable study of the novel has many new insights on the historical background of the novel, and on the psychology of Thomas Buddenbrook.

Ronald Peacock, *Das Leitmotiv bei Thomas Mann* (1934, Krauss reprint, 1970)

Eberhard Lämmert, 'Thomas Mann: *Buddenbrooks*' in: Benno von Wiese (ed.), *Der deutsche Roman. Vom Barock bis zur Gegenwart. Struktur und Gesellschaft*, vol. 2 (Düsseldorf, 1963), pp. 190–233

Jürgen Petersen, *Die Rolle, des Erzählers und die epische Ironie im Frühwerk Thomas Manns*, Dissertation (Cologne, 1967)

Herbert Lehnert, *Thomas Mann – Fiktion, Mythos, Religion* (Stuttgart, 1956)

Pierre-Paul Sagave, 'Zur Geschichtlichkeit von Thomas Manns Jugendroman: Bürgerliches Klassenbewußtsein und kapitalistische Praxis in *Buddenbrooks*', in: *Literaturwissenschaft*

und Geschichtsphilosophie. Festschrift für W. Emrich, Helmut
Arntzen (ed.) (Berlin, 1975), 436–52
Werner Frizen, *Zaubertrank der Metaphysik. Quellenkritische
Überlegungen im Umkreis der Schopenhauer-Rezeption Thomas
Manns*, Frankfurt am Main, Bern, Cirencester, 1980 (Europäische
Hochschulschriften)
Jochen Vogt, *Thomas Mann: 'Buddenbrooks'*, Text und
Geschichte, vol. 10 (Munich, 1983)

I also referred to Susanne Otto, *Literarische Produktion als egozentrische Variation des Problems von Identitätsfindung und -stabilisierung: Ursprung, Grundlagen und Konsequenzen bei Thomas Mann. Analyse des novellistischen Frühwerks mit Perspektive auf das Gesamtwerk* (Bern, 1982)

The question of the novel's social and historical placing has been much discussed in the German Democratic Republic. Lukács' essay on Mann is listed here, together with two short essays that summarise the discussion in the GDR.

Georg Lukács, 'Auf der Suche nach dem Bürger', in: *Deutsche Literatur in zwei Jahrhunderten* (Neuwied/Berlin, 1964), translated by S. Mitchell in: *Essays on Thomas Mann* (London, 1964)
Hans-Christian Oeser, 'The problematic nature of decline in Thomas Mann's novel *Buddenbrooks*', in *Universitas*, 22/2 (1980), 119–25
Michael Zeller, *Bürger oder Bourgeois? Eine literatursoziologische Studie zu Thomas Manns 'Buddenbrooks' und Heinrich Manns 'Im Schlaraffenland'* (Stuttgart, 1976)

Literary and social background

A reader wishing to know more of the literary and social background to the period in and about which Mann's novel was written may like to select from the following works:

Samuel Lublinski, *Die Bilanz der Moderne. Geistige Struktur um 1900*, G. Wunberg (ed.) (Tübingen, 1974)
Ernest K. Bramsted, *Aristocracy and the Middle-Classes in Germany. Social Types in German literature 1830/1900* (rev. ed. Chicago and London, 1964)
J. P. Stern, *Re-interpretations. Seven Studies in Nineteenth-Century German Literature* (London, 1964)
Walter Müller-Seidel, 'Literatur und Ideologie. Zur Situation des deutschen Romans um 1900', in: *Dichtung, Sprache, Gesellschaft*, V. Lange and H.-G. Roloff (ed.), (Frankfurt am Main, 1971), 593–602

Eda Sagarra, *Tradition and Revolution. German Literature and Society 1830/90* (London, 1971)
Roy Pascal, *From Naturalism to Expressionism. German Literature and Society 1880/1918* (London, 1973)
Karlheinz Rossbacher, *Heimatkunstbewegung und Heimatroman: Zu einer Literatursoziologie der Jahrhundertwende* (Stuttgart, 1975)

The last works illustrate the context of German literature in which *Buddenbrooks* appeared. More generally on realism, with occasional references to Mann:

Erich Auerbach, *Mimesis. The Representation of Reality in Western Literature* (Princeton, 1953)
F. W. J. Hemmings (ed.), *The Age of Realism* (Harmondsworth, 1974)
J. P. Stern, *On Realism* (London and Boston, 1973)

Three works were quoted directly on the relation between Mann and the modernist movement: the first an outstanding essay on the problems of the modern novel, the second a highly partisan essay and the third a recent and more literary-historical volume:

Theodor W. Adorno, 'Standort des Erzählers im zeitgenössischen Roman', in: *Noten zur Literatur I* (Frankfurt am Main, 1955), pp. 61ff.
Georg Lukács, 'Franz Kafka or Thomas Mann?' in: *The Meaning of Contemporary Realism*, translated by J. and N. Mander (London, 1962)
Malcolm Bradbury and James McFarlane, *Modernism 1890/1930* (Harmondsworth, 1976). This includes the essay: J. P. Stern, 'The theme of consciousness: Thomas Mann', pp. 416–29.

Two other works were quoted:

D. J. Enright, 'Aimez-vous Goethe? An enquiry into English attitudes of non-liking towards German Literature', in *Encounter*, 22 (1964), 93–7
Wilhelm Voßkamp, 'Gattungen als literarisch-soziale Einrichtungen', in: W. Hinck (ed.). *Textsortenlehre – Gattungsgeschichte* (Heidelberg, 1977), pp. 27–42

Early reviews of **Buddenbrooks**

Finally we list the early reviews of *Buddenbrooks* from which we have quoted. They are, like all ephemeral publications, not easily accessible, their authors interesting for the most part only as part of the voice of their age, and the reference is given for completeness only. Full bibliographical details are given in Harry Matter (*Die Literatur über Thomas Mann. Eine Bibliographie 1898/1969*, Berlin/Weimar, 1972) and for convenience we give here only the author and title of the essay, where Matter lists it:

Ernst Bertram, 'Das Problem des Verfalls' (1907)
Arthur Eloesser, 'Neue Bücher' (1901)
Otto Grautoff, '*Buddenbrooks*' (Jan. 1902)
Heinrich Hart, 'Neues vom Büchertisch' (1902)
Anselma Heine, '*Buddenbrooks*' (1901)
Eduard Korrodi, 'Thomas Mann', *Der Lesezirkel*, 1/5 (Jan. 1914), 89–94.
Hermann Anders Krüger, 'Romane', *Die schöne Literatur*, (18 Jan. 1902)
Franz Leppmann, '*Thomas Mann*' (1915)
Max Lorenz, '*Buddenbrooks*' (1902)
S. Lublinski, 'Thomas Mann: Die Buddenbrooks' (1902)
Henriette von Meerheimb, 'Neue Romane' (1904)
Elisabeth Neményi, '*Buddenbrooks*' (1903)
Leopold Schönhoff, 'Morituri' (1902)
Alois Stockmann, 'Die verbreitetesten Romane des letzten Jahres' (1904)
Richard Zimmermann, 'Lübeck im Roman der Gegenwart' (1910)